LIFE ON THE

HARD

SHOULDER

For Armchair Global Travelers, Backpackers, and Cycle Tourists

BY
Tony Thompson

Contents

Dedication

To my wife, Pauline, who supported me during my rides, it couldn't have been easy for her with me going away for months at a time.

My brothers and sisters and their families, thanks for always being supportive, so happy we all stayed close to each other, even if not in miles.

To Sue,
Many Thanks for your
support.
Enjoy this journey.
Tony

i

About The Author

Growing up in Grimsby, I was lucky to have had parents who truly cared about their children, and there were seven of us.

Leaving school just before my fifteenth birthday with a miserable tally of academic achievements, the pinnacle of my school career was being made a milk monitor. I hated school with teachers telling me I would never amount to anything; that's how to prepare children to face the world. When I look back at old photos, I was really small at fifteen, and shortly after leaving school, I shot up to over six feet. You don't need to have studied child development to draw any conclusion from that.

Unable to get a job, it was decided, against my father's wishes, that I might look towards becoming a priest or something in the church. I was sent to Gorton Monastery, Manchester a Franciscan friary, to explore whether this might be a way forward for me. The first thing to overwhelm me was this dimly lit Gothic silent place, and even worse was that the tea cups didn't have any handles! That night I was given a bed in a dormitory with other youngsters and forbidden to talk, watched over by a series of monks.

The following day, I walked out, never to return. I made it to the centre of Manchester. Here I met a group of homeless youngsters and learnt how to survive on the streets. We slept in one of the many derelict buildings around Piccadilly. One way to raise money was to offer people three pennies (1p) for a cigarette; they invariably just gave you the cigarette. There were always scruffy men around willing to buy them. After a while this life began to get boring and I knew I should let my family know I was OK. I hitchhiked home and was still unable to find work, I would hitchhike all over England, still selling cigarettes.

Finally, one guy gave me a job helping on a building site and I trained as a domestic plumber. Later moving on to larger projects, such as pipe fitting on the construction of power stations and oil refineries. This was a nomadic life living in digs and labour camps, which suited me perfectly.

I was always up for anything adventurous and learnt to parachute jump using the old WW2 surplus silk parachutes before the sports parachutes were invented. You had to climb out holding the wing strut and have one foot on the wheel, and then let go.

Figure 1 Three of Us Crammed Into A Cessna.

I used to run a sports club for people with a disability, I also dated a social worker who encouraged me to train to become a social worker as she thought "I was good with people.". After returning from South America, I applied to Southampton University and was accepted to complete a social work course, eventually becoming a manager in Social Services. I found I had a brain.

Throughout my working life, I ran my own business buying and restoring property, eventually building up a rental portfolio comprising thirty-eight properties in the UK, Spain, and the USA. This enabled me to travel for extended periods.

Acknowledgment

A special mention to Andy Pridmore, who uncomplainingly sorted out the mess I endlessly got into using the computer. Thank you.

"All the team at Fountains Cafe, Fair Oak, for their encouragement and support."

Foreword

You are welcome to join me on this trip back in time, but first, you need to know what's in store. What you won't get is how many miles I covered, a list of places, or endless facts and figures. Google can do that far better than I can. What you will get, and I hope to inspire others to travel by bicycle, are some of the adventures and mishaps I have encountered over the years.

To put my travels into some time frame, I'm writing this at the age of 78, which means most journeys were without any technological backup. Maps were paper, and contact with home was an occasional snail mail at "Poste Restante," but I did have a little cheap camera and rolls of film to be processed on my return. These photos have been kicking around in boxes for many years, and they were never the highest quality, but I hope they give some idea as to the situations I faced and the people I met. I carried a pen and a sketch pad with me and included a couple of my drawings.

Back then bank cards were not in use and you had to carry cash or Travellers Cheques, and hope that you were near a bank. I never had any problems, but always took protections such as I would take a 100 US Dollar note, roll it tightly in polythene and seal it with cellotape. Cutting a small slit on the inside of my shorts'/pants' waist band I could conceal my emergency stash of money.

In busy areas such as markets or train stations it is best to carry your backpack on your front otherwise you may get crowded out and your bag slashed. Women are more protected from having their breasts groped which is often not sexual but more a way of stopping you from protecting your valuables.

Finally trust your instinct.

I've changed some people's names, not to save them any embarrassment, but because I've forgotten what they are. Our travels together will take us across the USA, Canada, USSR, China, Australia, India, Nepal, Southeast Asia, Europe, Brazil, Argentina, and other countries. We'll lead two expeditions for people registered as blind into the oldest rain forest in the world to climb Gunung Tahan, the highest mountain in Peninsular Malaysia. We'll spend time growing potatoes in the Amazon Rain Forest. Escape from an Argentinian smuggling gang, get thrown out of a Thai massage parlour and arrested in China, and that's just for starters.

Can we take it as read that at some point, I got wet, cold, sunburnt, blown along, struggled against headwinds, and everything in between? People would often ask if I was ever scared of being alone and vulnerable on a bicycle. The scariest thing is the weather and motorists, as there is no reasoning with either of them. I did team up with a guy once, but not for long. He was constantly moaning, "It's so cold", "I'm so wet"," It's so steep" Did he think I hadn't noticed? Our teaming up didn't last for long, plus, being on my own, I can sing out loud. When you have such a bad voice as mine, it's only humane not to inflict it on others. My repertoire is "I was born under a wandering star", "Been through a desert on a bike with no name", (sic), and "On the road again".

I make no apologies for using both miles and kilometres because that is what you are faced with on the road.

My Obsession with Travelling

Growing up in Grimsby, a once bustling deep sea fishing town with the crews known as "two-day millionaires" while having a two-day break before setting off for the icy waters of the North Sea and in the Arctic Circle. My ambition was to work on a trawler, however this was thwarted when "The Icelandic Cod wars" flared up again and anyone under 16 was not allowed to sail. I had a job down at the docks before school and would spend time listening and talking to the trawler men recounting their adventures in towns across the North Sea. It was hardly surprising that I wanted to travel.

My two heroes in school were Swaby, who had been to France on a day trip, and Bishop, whose dad was stationed in Germany. Those poor kids. I constantly asked them what it was like in another country and made Bishop endlessly recite the few words in German he knew. No wonder they would run off when they saw me coming. We lived two doors from Dod Orsborne, who was skipper of a Grimsby fishing boat, the "Girl Pat", which he stole, and using a 6d (2.5p) atlas from Woolworths, crossed the Atlantic, eventually going on to have many adventures around the world before being arrested. I grew up listening to tales about him.

At 15, I took my first solo venture by train to Yugoslavia, carrying everything I needed in two paper carrier bags. After crossing the border, I encountered armed border guards in what was then a communist country. My eyes were so wide that one of them nearly fell out. Store that information as you'll need it later. OK, let's head off, initially not by bicycle.

Chapter 1: Mexico and South America 1980

I landed in Los Angeles and took a couple of days just outside to get over the jet lag. Borrowing a fishing rod, I set up at the end of a pier next to which a grey whale beached itself next to the pier. After a short while, several dolphins started bumping into the whale, refloating it. The whale took off, skimming the pier I was on and close enough to touch. My fishing line was still over the side and hooked the whale's side as it went past. The line snapped, nevertheless I am claiming, maybe spuriously, the record for the biggest fish that got away.

We are looking at a time before South America became a well-travelled backpacker route or "Gringo Trails".

From Tijuana, Mexico I planned to take a coach to Mexico City. To ensure I didn't miss the bus and I was sure of a seat, I queued up first, but as the coach pulled in, I received my first lesson in Mexican etiquette. Suddenly I was being buffeted on all side by dozens of little round "Abuelita's" or grannies. I ended up last on the coach sitting next to a larger-than-life Mexican woman with bright red hair, bright red clothes, makeup, and shoes to match for two days. She kindly took me under her ample wing, ensuring I was OK at every service stop. Feeding me throughout the journey with some soft sweets, which she assured me would help the trip go quicker. It wasn't until well into the second day I realised that to make them nice and soft, she actually chewed them first. I survived.

I flew to Bogota and onto Quito in Ecuador. It's best not to use hand signals until you know the country well. One American guy who wanted to show his appreciation, thanked a local guy by making the letter O sign with his thumb and first finger, not realising that in Ecuador that means you are calling him an A-hole.

Taking the light railway from Quito at 2,850 meters to sea level at Guayaquil, the rail took us through the canopy of the rain forest down to floor level and into farm land. This train no longer seems to exist which is a shame.

On a 1,500 km coach trip from Guayaquil to Lima I met Lucia who introduced me to life in the Amazon rainforest and probably had the most profound influence on me for future travels. She was a researcher at Lima University and her specialty was potatoes. Peru has so many different strains of potato, they hold a special place in their culture. Her project was researching the best kind of potato to grow in the Amazon rainforest, primarily along the deltas and tributaries of the Ucayali River. This was seen to be necessary because of the poor diet of the local population.

Lucia asked if I would like to accompany her from Lima to Pucallpa and visit some of her projects—a two-day journey on some of the worst tracks across the Andes to Pucallpa.

Figure 2 Crossing the Andes

At one point, the passengers had to get off and push the coach away from the side of a very long drop. Pucallpa was an interesting town back then, it reminded me of the old Cowboy films I watched as a child. Mud roads with wooden sidewalks and largely wooden buildings with a busy port, it was the last navigable town directly connected to the River Amazon and the outside world. Small wooden commercial vessels plied their trade, bringing in goods collected from larger ships that had travelled from all over the world, now moored at the mouth of the Amazon. These goods are then taken by trucks to Lima. It was a viable and quicker path than ships taking the longer route through the Panama Canal.

Pucallpa had an interesting transient population made up of prospectors, gamblers, prostitutes and dealers in the illegal trade of hardwood trees and drugs. I was told it was also a place to come if you wanted to stay out of the arms of law enforcement. Drug dealers smuggling cocaine into Brazil came from Tingo Marie, which was a well-known centre for the cartels. We stopped there on our way from Lima, where I was warned not to leave the bus depot due to the drug gangs' deep suspicion of gringos. Apparently, the USA had DEA (Drug Enforcement Agency) agents regularly posing as backpackers "nosing around."

Lucia took me to a smaller village, Yarinacocha, on the banks of the river, which was where the university had her base. We stayed with Georgio, Elizabeth and their three children. Georgio owned a long tail boat, and was paid to ferry various members of the university staff to the villages where the different strains of potatoes were being grown. He also had to ensure that University Staff had food and accommodation. Lucia asked if I wanted to be involved and said that all I had to do was go with Georgio, visit the various villages, and make notes as to how the crop was doing. Being

3

brought up in Lincolnshire, maybe she had unrealistic expectations about my knowledge of potatoes. Over the next few months, I really didn't see very many people from the University, and any that came didn't hang around. I made notes on how many and how big the shoots were and after each circuit of the villages, I gave Georgio my reports and he sent them back to Lucia in Lima. I never saw her or heard from her again.

Figure 3 Good Job Giorgio Knew The Way.

Living in the villages and getting to know the people has been one of the highlights of my life. Walking through a village, I would feel a little hand gently rubbing up my arm and then children giggling and running away. The local people didn't have bodily hair, so the children were fascinated by this tall, hairy man. Although Georgio always left me plenty of food, I would try to catch fish, the children taught me how to spear fish. The spear consisted of a long handle with three prongs on the end. You had to stand in the river with the tips just under the surface; this counteracted the effect of refraction. Needless to say, I was a complete failure, much to the enjoyment and merriment of all the children. However, I did eventually catch a fish and the children were so pleased that they paraded me and my fish through the village to the delight of the adults with a lot of shouting and more laughter.

Sometime later, one of the villagers brought me a live piranha fish, which was not very big but surprisingly colourful. I never took any photos of the people as it felt like an intrusion. I placed the piranha on a log, to photograph it, but it kept flapping about and, in an effort to stop it I put my hand too close to its mouth and it took a chunk out of my finger. So, there's another spurious boast of mine about being attacked by piranha in the Amazon.

Going to bed one evening I went to my hut only to find a visitor fast asleep in there. Hanging from the roof structure was a sloth; it stayed there for two days and nights without moving; the villagers made out that I shouldn't worry it was a common occurrence. I was thrilled, although I had concerns that it might pee on me in the night. But it didn't. My other contact with a sloth came in a clearing where I had sat down on a log for a break; I was walking to the next village. Out of the undergrowth appeared a sloth walking on all fours toward me; it was clearly on a mission and not hanging around. When it was within a couple of feet, I thought he was not going to go round me, so I moved out of the way. The sloth continued straight over the log where I had been sitting and away into the undergrowth. I often wonder if I hadn't moved, would it have just walked over me?

The river is the life blood of all these villages, and I was fortunate to go out with the men fishing and hunting along the waterways. Regular sightings of caiman of all sizes, they are related to crocodile/alligator and are just as dangerous. After sundown, occasionally, I would go down to the water's edge with a torch looking for caiman, all you would see were two bright red eyes like glowing cigarettes, very slowly, the caiman would slide away backwards into the river.

All your ablutions are done in the river with a warning not to put your feet down because of the electric eels. Swimming out into the middle, I found what looked like an island but was, in fact, thousands of mosquitoes resting before their onslaught as the sun went down. My first night I had so many bites that my whole back was covered. The only way I could protect myself was to wear my plastic kagool with the hood up and a piece of rag to swat mosquitoes off my legs. However, I would mostly get into bed early with the mosquito net firmly in place.

Georgio had a sideline of meeting the bus from Lima and persuading any westerners who ventured so far into staying at his place. He would take them on trips down the river visiting a village. He asked me to accompany him as his English was not too good. One group we took out included a German guy who spent the time boring everyone with his tales of fishing and how good he was. As it happened a medium size fish jumped onto the back of the boat. I motioned Georgio not to say anything. Picking the fish up I clamped it in my teeth and slid overboard. Coming up at the front I let the fish go into the boat and said to the German guy "now that's how to catch fish". He was impressed and told me later he had written about how I caught a fish in my mouth underwater in his journal. And another one of my spurious claims,

One village was having a ceremony and I was given a tiny drop of ayahuasca, to this day I don't have a clue what happened or how I got to bed. Never tried that again. After several months living in the Amazon rainforest, I had lost so much weight and was beginning to feel weak so decided I had to sadly leave and head over the Andes back to Lima.

Back in the UK I was a volunteer with the Hampshire Association for the Care of the Blind, HACB and the manager Jo heard about my plan to visit Lima and said she knew her counterpart there and that I should contact her. This I did and was asked if I would meet up with Camila, a young woman who was training to be an English teacher and translator. This would give her a chance to practice talking to a native English speaker. I arranged to meet up with Camila and her fiancée Henry. Hang on to Henry, we will meet him again. The three of us spent an afternoon in the museum where Henry would read the label on the exhibit and Camila would translate for me. I won't go into how many mummified bodies that are exhibited but if I never see another it will be too soon. I hope Camila found it helpful.

I met some young guys who had built their own hang gliders and invited me to head out into the Atacama Desert to watch them fly. Some were ok, if heavy and not lifting off very high. But the desert was interesting.

Figure 4 Flying Over Atacama Desert

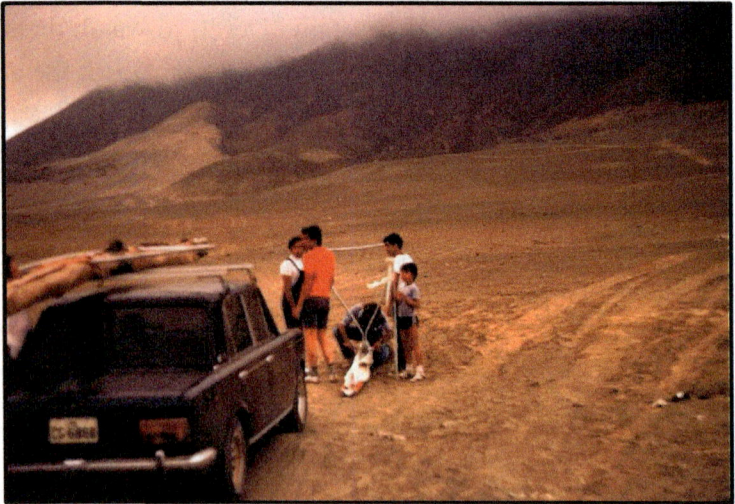
Figure 5 Second Thoughts About Using Homemade Hang Gilders

Leaving Lima I town hopped along the Andes and standing out as a foreigner always found someone to talk to. One topic that men wanted to talk about was football. All thanked England for inventing the game and I usually got a thumbs up. It was in a remote town in the Andes that I was told that the English international Kevin Keagan had joined my football team Southampton, which was so highly unlikely I didn't believe it. It was several months before I returned to the UK that I found out it was true. Amazing!

Sitting drinking coffee in another town, a local stopped and said that he wanted to thank me as a German company had installed television in the valley. I couldn't take credit for that so I told him I was English, to which he reacted by standing up straight, making a Nazi salute, shouted, "Heil Hitler" and stormed off.

I met Rosa Poma in Huan Cayo, a local TV star with a flamboyant personality and always plenty to say. She had very distinct features and told me she was descendant from the Incas. Always dressed in bright clothes, she was recognised wherever she went. We will meet Rosa again in England.

Figure 6 Rosa Poma

Moving onto the city of Cusco and on the trek up to Machu Picchu is where I was introduced to chewing unprocessed coca leaves, these are used by the locals and legal above 11,152 ft. It helps with altitude sickness and tiredness.

My next destination was La Paz in Bolivia. En route I met an English woman whose husband was a captain in the Peruvian Navy, presently stationed on Lake Titicaca were the border between Peru and Bolivia splits the lake in two. She said she would ask her husband if I could join them on a trip out into the lake. As always people are wonderfully accommodating and I got to visit several of the reed-built islands. Even joining in with some boys in a game of football. A very weird sensation running on the floating reed surface which was a bit like walking on a soft mattress.

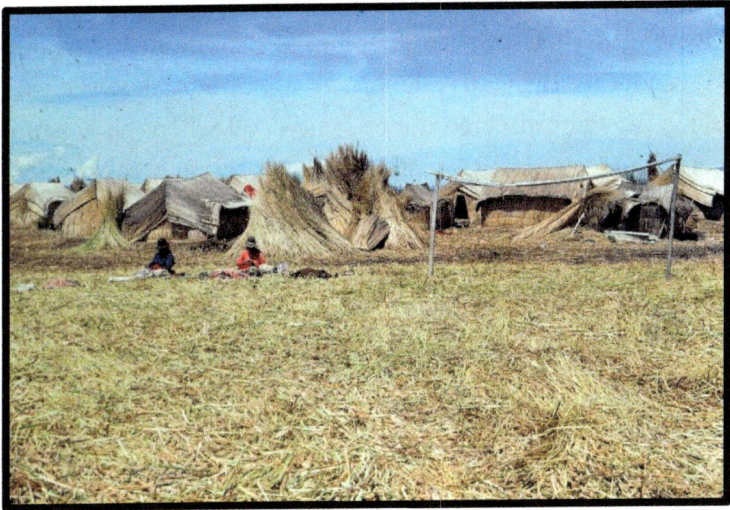

Figure 7 Football Pitch on Lake Titicaca

If the Captain had known about my reputation as a Jonah, which we will look into later, he would not have let me on board. Sure enough half way through the patrol they ran out of diesel! We drifted sedately for an hour or so until a relief vessel came out with diesel and we were on our way with a somewhat red-faced crew.

Moving onto La Paz, Bolivia where the joke is that oxygen levels are so low nothing burns and therefore don't need a fire brigade. The day I arrived I was advised by the hostel manager not to go out in the evening because of demonstrations against the government and reportedly a local priest had been hung from a lamp-post earlier that day, not too sure if this was correct but they do have a history of hanging people including priests from lamp-posts. In traveller's hostels there are logs where you can leave messages for others, such as where to visit and what to avoid. I came across an entry from Jack, an English man, incarcerated in La Paz's notorious prison, San Pedro, asking if any travellers could visit and bring things like soap, shampoo etc. I visited the next day and apart from leaving my passport and camera at the entrance was allowed to just wander in. Basically, the prison was run by the prisoners. An American prisoner directed me to Jack's cell where he was pleased to receive the toiletries. I spent three hours there, he explained how he and his wife had been arrested at the airport with a kilo of cocaine each. He believed they had been set up by the seller and the police.

They had been in prison for almost two years still waiting to go to trial. His wife was locked in a local nunnery and was allowed to visit him once a month. He relied on his family to send him money via the British Consulate which was used to "rent" a single cell and for food. The alternative was an overcrowded communal cell holding dozens of prisoners and was dangerous. He showed me a huge scar on his back from being stabbed soon after arriving in the prison. The prison itself contained some of the most notorious drug gangs and fights between them was not unusual. Some enterprising prisoners had set up small businesses such as food stalls, barbers and even a brothel, open on visiting days when women claiming to be relatives could visit the prison. I never saw a guard and the prison gangs policed their own areas. I was introduced to other westerners, all from USA, there for drug offences. However, there was something to celebrate, a letter from a former inmate, dressed as a woman who had escaped by climbing over a roof and into the street beyond.

My next destination was Argentina and a coach ride of 24 hours to Salta. Arriving in Salta I went in search of a place to stay and was approached by two guys who introduced themselves as police and I was to accompany them to the police station. After a thorough search of me and my things – finding nothing, I was then informed just how easy it was to find some cocaine in my backpack. That invariably led to years in jail just waiting to go to trial. Clearly, I had little money so a bribe was out of the question.

They went on to explain that due to hyperinflation buying anything locally was extremely expensive. The joke at the time was that you should pay when ordering a meal in a restaurant or your bill would have doubled in price by the end of the meal. The police officers plan was to go to Santa Cruz in Bolivia where the sales tax was very low. To ensure no cocaine was found on me I needed to go with them where they would buy goods and providing a foreign national, who are exempt from paying any import tax, could take them into Argentina. The officers promised to pay all my expenses and buy me a ticket to Paraguay from Salta. Very kindly they agreed to look after my passport until I got on the coach to Paraguay, to ensure it was safe. What could go wrong? Well, they had failed to tell me that all the goods I was to bring into Argentina would be listed in my passport and if I failed to take them out of the country, I would be liable to pay the tax. I had been explained all this when I first crossed into Argentina and my camera had been noted inside my passport. I knew I could not return with them and face a crippling import tax or jail for smuggling.

That evening, six policemen, out of uniform, and I boarded a coach to Bolivia. We checked into a cheap hotel in Santa Cruz and over the next three days I was kept in the room and guarded by one of them at gunpoint. During which time they went on a shopping spree and slowly my room filled up with a myriad of items from books to electrical goods. On the fourth day I was going stir crazy and acting weird, crying and shouting, banging things loudly. Basically, acting weird, half acting and half for real, at being couped up and not knowing quite how to get out of the situation. One of them lent me a tape recorder with a Simon and Garfunkel's greatest hits tape. Even now over forty years on if one of those tracks comes on the radio it takes me straight back to that horrible little room. They eventually agreed I could go out for a walk accompanied by two of the men, fortunately neither could speak English. Remember Henry from Lima? To my amazement there he was walking towards me across the Plaza De 24 September (the date they celebrate a popular revolt that took place in 1810) It turns out that Henry was a traveling sales rep with a greetings card company and he has several customers in Santa Cruz. I explained my plight much to the discomfort of my body guards who didn't have a clue what was going on. Henry assured me he had friends in the Bolivian Police force and they enjoyed arresting Argentinian police. No idea why! Henry told me that they would come and get me that evening. Sure enough Henry turned up with several armed police demanding to see everyone's ID including my passport, which they found was out of order. I was to accompany them to the police station. I wish I could have had a picture of the Argentinians faces now stuck with a large amount of luxury goods and no second plan as to how to avoid the crippling tax on imports. The local police and Henry escorted me to the train station where I was shown a seat and Henry gave me a ticket to San Paulo in Brazil. The police and Henry remained on the platform until the train pulled out. I suspect Henry had paid for the ticket and any bribes but he waved away my offer to pay.

One of the passengers informed me I was on the Tren de Muerte or the Death Train. I assumed that for the duration I needed to be extra vigilant. Sometime later I discovered it was named not because it was dangerous but it was used many years previously to transport victims of the yellow fever outbreak to camps outside the towns and their bodies to special burial sites. It was surprisingly slow but fascinating and while crossing the Mato Grosso the train jumped the tracks, clearly not an unusual occurrence as jacks etc. were produced and they had the engine back on track after a couple of hours. Impressive if slow. I never heard from Henry again and lost contact, the down side of travel pre technology.

Figure 8 Tren de Morte

Sao Paulo is Brazil's commercial powerhouse and extremely crowded and busy. I took the next coach to Rio de Janeiro where they were clearly expecting me, with a huge banner over the main road proclaiming "WELCOME TONY". I was told it was meant for Tony Bennett's tour in 1980. Huh, I was taking it anyway, yes another of my spurious claims to fame.

A cheap hotel close to Flamengo Beach was a perfect place for some relaxation after several days on the Death Train. Walking along the beach, before long you would be invited to join in one of the many impromptu games of football played on the public football fields.

My first night in Rio I wandered down to the beach where there were many small fires lit. Great, I thought of beach parties. Oh no, this was a celebration to Yemanja, the Goddess of the seas so I made a quick exit. I had no experience of Blackmagic and would often see little offerings to various deities, including one for smokers in and around Rio. Mara, one of the hotel's staff, invited me to join her and others from the hotel to go to the Maracana Stadium and watch their team Flamengo play. I attended several games and it was the season Zico led them to the championship.

Loved Rio, the craziest city I have ever visited and that's coming from someone who prefers to be out in the country. You really don't even contemplate going out before mid-night. I soon found out why discos had floor to ceiling mirrors, the young women liked to watch themselves dancing and sooner or later most of the girls removed their tops. Not one to generally visit discos, I decided to make an effort in this case, as after all traveling is about learning what goes on in other cultures. I got into a conversation with a local man, who when I told him that the pubs in UK closed at 10.30, he could not comprehend anything like that and basically thought I was lying. And my cred sank even lower when he found it amazing, I hadn't had sex with a Brazilian girl yet, despite being in the country for less than 24 hours.

Moving on from Rio and heading north the towns proved to be just as crazy with one or two wild nights. One stands out and after spending a night with one girl we arranged to meet the following

16

afternoon. It was only then I realised she only had one arm, I just hadn't noticed. The result of a car accident as a child.

My plan was to take a river boat at Belem and sail up the River Amazon to Manaus. I took a small cabin rather than buy a hammock and struggle to find a couple of hooks on the lower deck, which was absolutely crammed with people and animals. I got to know a couple of Argentinian men, a gay couple, escaping from their home country where they were persecuted. Well, escaping from Argentina we had at least that much in common. The boat stopped at many small towns or villages along the river loading and unloading all manner of goods and people. After one stop the two guys bought me an ash tray made locally. They said it was because I treated and related to them as "humans". I still treasure it today. One crazy night the two put on a cabaret show on deck with some amazing dancing and costumes. All in the middle of the Amazon jungle. It wasn't the last weird night spent at one of the river towns where they had a dance floor. Among the usual Brazilian rock music, I heard for the first time "Another Brick in the Wall." By Pink Floyd. Wow!

I don't know what happened to my Argentinian friends once we reached Manaus but I guess they didn't frequent the kind of bars that I headed for. Manaus was my final destination in South America and I flew home via LA, reflecting on how my travels had been and the many hours of misery crammed in those small, uncomfortable coach seats, desperate for a pee the moment I got on and watching all the interesting places we would race through. It was on the flight home I decided to give cycling a go.

Back home in England, Rosa wrote to me saying she was coming to England and arriving the following week. Arriving at Heathrow wearing a bright yellow Stetson, red waistcoat and white jeans saying her goodbyes to half the other passengers who all seemed to know her. Not one to hide in a crowd!

It was a difficult time for me as I was in the process of ripping apart a property I had just bought ready to renovate. I'm fine living amongst the rubble with basic amenities which is why I suggested we take a camping trip in the New Forest. Rosa had never been in a tent and was really up for it. That evening we visited a local pub where Rosa was instantly the centre of attention with her primary-coloured clothes and her vivacious personality. As we were leaving Rosa announced "I am so excited, tonight is my first time" resulting in several men choking on their beer. I should have explained she was talking about camping, but I didn't. Later that night Rosa was still talking non-stop prompting me to remark "Rosa you don't half rabbit on", a mistake on my part as I then had to explain to her that rabbiting on meant talking nonstop.

Next evening same pub, same locals, same Rosa holding court. Time came to leave and clearly most of the bar wanted to know how was Rosa's "first time". With several pints inside him one guy feeling brave could not resist and shouted, "Rosa how was your first time?" Rosa replied, "Oh, Tony make a joke with me, he said I go like a rabbit". We left the pub to the sound of several people choking on their drinks. Oh, the pitfalls of speaking a foreign language without having a background of the colloquialisms.

Chapter 2: The Bike

The dream of travelling by bike was starting to come to fruition. Over the years I used three-way different bikes. Falcon, Dean, and lastly a Surly Long-Haul Trucker.

I rode the Falcon around southern Ireland as a trial. With a few additions, such as Kevlar strips inside the tyres as a precaution against punctures, and steel racks front and rear—although lighter alloy ones were becoming available—I wanted to be able to have them welded back together if they broke under the weight I was planning to carry. Everything had to be easily fixed, so I chose imperial-sized wheels and tyres after finding out that metric sizes might not be available in places like Asia in general.

Cycle helmets were not something you considered back then—I'm not even sure they were readily available. A rear-view mirror became a 100% must, as whenever I tried to look over my shoulder, I ended up wobbling all over the road. I told the owner of the local bike shop that I planned to cycle to Singapore, he looked me and my bike up and down and, sneeringly, said, "I doubt if you'll make it to the end of the road." I put his remark down to him being a snobby racer. Fortunately, I did get round the first corner before falling off.

As years went by, I swapped to Schwalbe Continental tyres, virtually puncture resistant. The only thing that ever went through them was the high tensile steel wire from a vehicle tyre that had been shredded.

My last bike was a Surly Long-Haul Trucker. This has a stretched frame, perfect for tall riders and I no longer "heeled" my pannier bags.

Chapter 3: Europe, Turkey, Cyprus and Rhodes

I took the ferry from Ramsgate to Ostend and decided that was enough for my first day and went in search of a campsite. Fully loaded I soon gained the attention of Belgians, who love cycling. How pleased I was telling anyone around me that I was riding all the way to Singapore. With an interesting crowd looking on I started putting up my new tent. Basic mistake, it was the one thing I had not unpacked since buying it or had a trial run. I was trying to erect it inside out. I couldn't understand what they were saying but I'm sure it was similar to the bike shop owner "I doubt if he'll make it to the corner". I learned my lesson about showing off!

It didn't take me long once I started getting into the Alps, to realise that I really was carrying too much and so I played a little game with myself. The rule was that every time I stopped, I had to discard something. One sock at a time didn't really make sense, after all what was the use of an odd sock, but that didn't stop me. I headed for Ljubljana to meet up with my girlfriend, a senior physiotherapist, who was on an exchange with a hospital in Ljubljana.

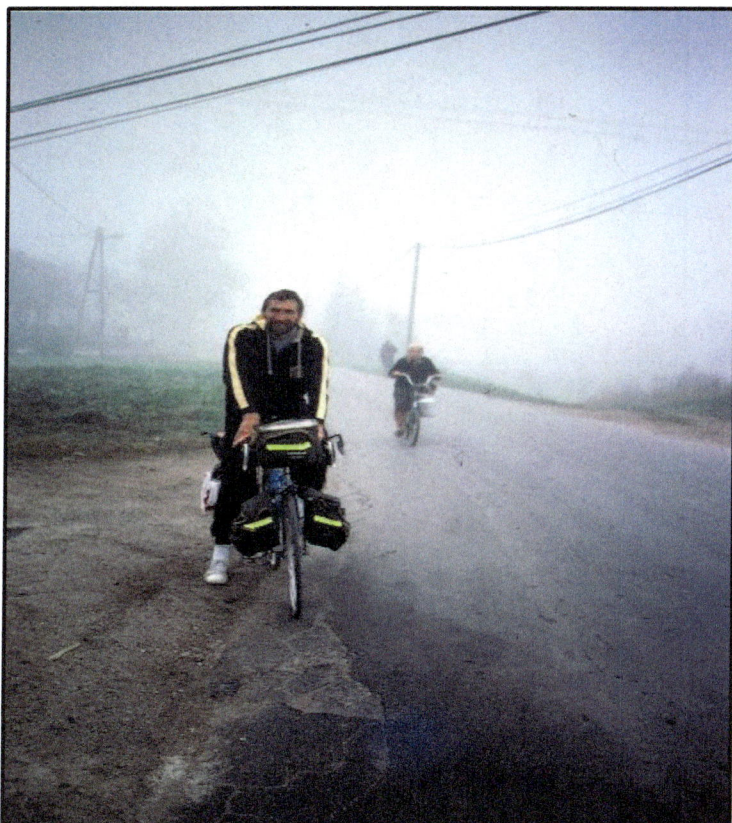

Figure 9 Leaving Ljubljana

On to Zagreb, and through Serbia to Belgrade. From there through the Rhodope Mountains. When reaching the brow of one of the passes I looked up and realised about twenty feet above me was a pack of wolves keeping pace with me. I have to admit I was glad that I was at the top and I didn't even contemplate braking on the way down. I didn't see them again.

Figure 10 Cold and Wet.

Going through Bulgaria and passing a small farm I stopped to watch the whole family busy brewing pure alcohol from plums. Invited to join and sample their brew was a mistake as I found out when trying to get back on the bike.

Apart from the wolves it was fairly uneventful but a very enjoyable scenic cycle ride. Wherever I stopped I was met with such friendly people, one "baba" loaded me down with jars of pickled vegetables. Hard to believe that only a few years earlier The Croatian War of Independence had been raging.

On this stretch, the tents main telescopic fibreglass pole broke and until I reached Istanbul, where my girlfriend posted me a replacement, I had to jury rig the tent every night, and not always successfully keeping the rain out.

Figure 11 Jury Rigged Tent

The weather improved when I reached the Greek border where I was delighted to see the border guards wearing the traditional Evzones uniform. Dropping down towards the coast, I was wet and cold. A sign on the side of the road advertised a hot natural pool, just what I needed, only to reach the entrance to see another sign saying "closed". Nothing can express the disappointment, and feeling sorry for myself when a car pulled up with the owner and his family, they took one look at the state of me and invited me in. I was shown to the hot pool and the owner took my kit away to get it dried. I had found nirvana. Before I left the couple served up a huge plate of moussaka. Life was pretty good once again.

I dropped down to the coast, at last the weather improved and I had a very pleasant if rugged ride through small towns keeping to local roads. I eventually had to go inland to reach the border crossing to Turkey. At some point I had to join the E90, a major trucking route which I did not want to be on, having avoided these routes since leaving the UK. About a mile from the border, I climbed over a barrier onto the main road to join the trucks, fortunately nearing the border the trucks came to a standstill joining a queue. There is something special about being on a bike able to sail past all those juggernauts and getting friendly cheers from the drivers.

Figure 12 Help to Have A Shower.

Once into Turkey I decided to follow the main route as it had a good wide shoulder and service stations which didn't object to me camping out the back. Unfortunately, there were packs of feral dogs that didn't attack me, but it was disconcerting being in the tent with these dogs sniffing around and growling all night.

Leaving Istanbul, a most intriguing city, I followed the coast road. Dropping down into small fishing towns was definitely a highlight, especially the food. While in Turkey, I camped in various ancient ruins, the most famous being the city of Troy, where they have a full-size wooden Trojan Horse. Marmaris being my final Turkish destination with a plan to take a ferry to Rhodes and then onto Cyprus. Before that however, I wanted to visit Cappadocia inland, and I can honestly say my first sight of those conical shaped mounds where people had carved out the interiors and made their homes. was truly breathtaking. A must for any traveller.

Figure 13 Cappadocia

After taking the ferry from Marmaris to Rhodes, I had a very pleasant two-day trip around the island, sleeping in one of the many ancient ruins and letting my imagination run wild, thinking of the people who had slept there over the last several centuries. Another ferry ride took me to Cyprus, where I felt at home as they drive on the left-hand side of the road and have road signage like that in the UK. My final ferry ride took me to Haifa in Israel, where you needed to ask passport control not to stamp your passport if you intended to travel to any Muslim countries.

Chapter 4: Israel & Gaza

A pleasant ride along the coast road to Tel Aviv and once again, people were extremely kind. I was invited to stay the night with a family. I'm not sure I endeared myself to them, as they kindly offered to wash my clothes, including a red jumper I had bought in a market in Bulgaria. I wasn't concerned about my clothes taking on a red hue, but they put their white bedding in after me, and there was clearly red dye still in the machine, turning their bedding a wonderful shade of pink.

As always, I tried to stay off the main roads, and the back road to Jerusalem had some tough climbs, still preferable to the busy dual carriageway.

Jerusalem! Wow, absolutely fascinating, but definitely with an undercurrent, as neither Jews, Muslims, nor Christians were particularly comfortable with each other, especially around places such as the Temple Mount, claimed as a holy place by all three religions. Leaving Jerusalem and heading for the Dead Sea, travel became tougher in respect of finding water and food, as the local population live communally in kibbutzim's, generally some distance from the main road and surrounded by high chain-link fences. However, I was never turned away and had a couple of very pleasant evenings being fed and given a bed for the night.

Dropping down to the Dead Sea, I was surprised to see so many people having a great time on the beaches, as it was Shavuot holiday. Of course, I had to have a dip in the water—that's all you can do, as swimming is virtually impossible. Hardly surprising there weren't any lifeguards. They all had so much food left over at the end of the day, which I was pleased to stock up on, as I was told there was nothing on my planned route to Be'er Sheva. Just to remind myself,

I am writing about things that took place over forty-five years ago—I believe there are hotels along the Dead Sea Road now.

Leaving the Dead Sea behind, there is a long, slow haul of 50 miles through the arid desert to Be'er Sheva. Reaching the top of the climb away from the Dead Sea, I was met at the scenic lookout by motorists applauding me. How very embarrassing. At least I could top up my water bottles. Before reaching Be'er Sheva, I set up camp at the side of the road just as it was getting dark. About an hour after the sun went down, the military arrived, fully armed and shouting at me to crawl out—well, you don't have much choice in those tents. Once they had established who I was and what I was doing there, they insisted I could not stay and that about ten miles further on was a petrol station where I should camp instead. That ten miles in the dark was not my idea of fun, as despite having a rear light, I had become invisible to motorists, who, I suspect, had been down on the beach enjoying their kosher wine.

Fully loaded with snacks and water, I left Be'er Sheva early in the morning, heading for the checkpoint at Erez and hopefully being allowed into Gaza

Gaza

Crossing into Gaza was no problem, although I was asked if I had ever been to Israel! Where else could I have been? I was shown the same hospitality by the Palestinian people as I had everywhere else, being allowed to sleep in one man's garage, where he went to a lot of trouble to rig up an electric light bulb for me. What was most striking for me was how there was no difference between the aspirations of those on both sides of the border—just wanting to do

27

the best for their families. It is heartbreaking to see the destruction of Gaza going on in 2024/25.

Chapter 5: Egypt and the Eastern Desert

Following the north Egyptian Sinai desert road from Rafah to Al-Arish and on to Bir al-Abd, I felt uncomfortable for the first time, as there seemed to be a low level of suspicion towards me. Throughout my travels, I have listened to my instincts, and although I had planned to stay there that night, I decided to move on. I had particularly wanted to travel this coast road, imagining what my father must have had to deal with, weather- and terrain-wise, during the war as he and his comrades headed towards Lebanon.

Figure 14 Company Along the Road

A reasonably uneventful few days led me to Cairo. The landscape changed from desert to farmland the closer I got to the River Nile, and traffic became increasingly busy as I neared the city, with no seeming sense of who had the right of way or which side of the road you were meant to be on. Once in Cairo, the traffic chaos got even worse, and I hit what was left of a metal post sticking up in the middle of the road.

Physically, I was OK, but a split in my tyre was not welcome. Fortunately, it wasn't hard to replace, plus I carried a spare. Staying at a rat-infested travellers' hostel in the centre of Cairo didn't endear me to the city, and I couldn't leave quickly enough. After visiting the Sphinx, where I was surrounded by small boys all trying to open my panniers bags and managing to steal some shampoo from one of the pockets. I moved on swiftly to the Pyramids of Giza.

On reaching the pyramids, I noticed an enclosure which I figured might be a good place to leave my bike while I looked around. Fortunately, it was being used by some American and Egyptian archaeologists who were X-raying the pyramids, searching for tunnels or more tombs. They said I could camp in the enclosure that night. At sundown, the Egyptian police cleared all the tourists and locals selling souvenirs or camel rides out of the area. As I already had a penchant for camping in ancient sites, I figured this would be the Holy Grail and set up my tent between two of the pyramids.

Just as I was about to drop off to sleep, my tent was suddenly lit up. "Oh, ****" I thought. "The police are up here checking things out, and they're probably going to move me on." The thought of trying to ride somewhere in the dark through the outskirts of Cairo filled me with dread. I waited for the inevitable shaking of the tent. After a few minutes—nothing. What was going on? Hesitantly, I looked out of my tent door and soon realised I was in the middle of the son et lumière, with the audience down below by the Sphinx. I must have been so small next to the pyramids that no one noticed me.

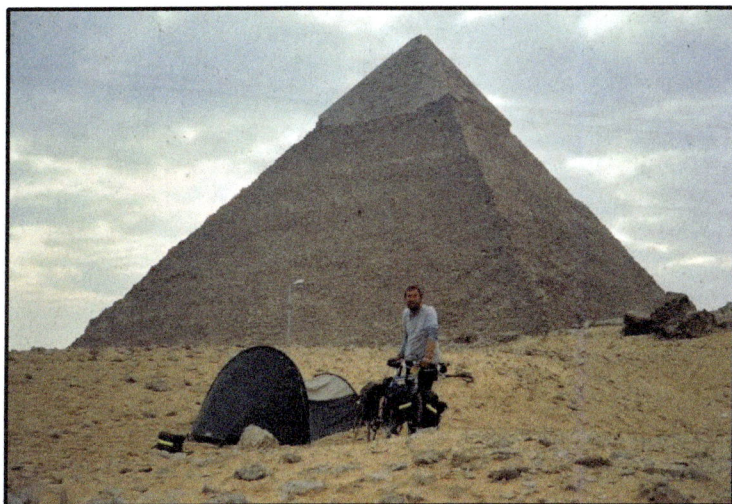

Figure 15 Not an Approved Camp Site.

Leaving Cairo and heading up towards Luxor the road out was the busiest most dangerous road I have been on, very narrow with huge trucks all being overtaken by cars and vans. I passed a worrying number of wrecks abandoned just off the road. On my left was desert and between the road and the River Nile was all farm land. There had to be farm tracks and sure enough I was able to continue in relative peace alongside the Nile on baked hard mud tracks. Several small towns along the way for food and always a peaceful place to set up camp or a cheap hotel, in one I woke up to the miserable sight and discomfort of having been eaten alive by bed bugs. It took a long time to find and eradicate them, which I did once I found an isolated spot where I could strip off. About 700 km and a ferry crossing, to reach Luxor. It was a delightful journey, apart from one small stretch of desert where ahead was a man on a donkey, nothing else to be seen, as I passed him, he suddenly pulled the donkeys' head left to turn and I crashed into him. We were both OK.

31

Figure 16 The Man and Donkey I Ran Into!

From Luxor I rode out to the Valley of Kings feeling rather superior on my bright red bike while all the other tourists clonked along on locally rented wrecks. That was until I got a puncture and realised I had left my spare tube back in the hotel. Not so smug now was I.

At this time my plan was to follow the Nile up into Ethiopia. However, the word was that the border was closed because of the civil war raging there. My only alternative was to head back to Israel and take a flight to India. Not wanting to retrace my ride along the Nile I tried to find out if I could get across the Eastern Desert to the El Quseir Marsa Alam Road that ran alongside the Red Sea and the Suez Canal. Back then there was no road across the Eastern Desert, however, I was told that a recent fresh water pipe line had been laid to feed the area around Safaga, a small town on the Red Sea and I could follow that. Half way I would come across an engineer's encampment where I could at least get water and continue following the pipe line.

Crossing the Eastern Desert.

Well of course what could be difficult cycling in the desert? My progress was a cross between cycling and when the sand got too soft dragging all my stuff plus several litres of water through the sand! One tough section I abandoned my bike yelling at it in Basil Fawlty style, "That's it! You've been warned about sinking in the sand. I'm leaving you here!" I marched of and looked back at my poor pathetic bike and started laughing at how ludicrous it all was. Maybe the heat might have had something to do with it?

Figure 17 I Had Warned the Bike It Would Get Left Behind If It Continually Got Sunk In The Sand!

Just before the sun goes down when it gets really cold, my routine was to cook and eat something outside. Get into my sleeping bag and light a candle, balance it on my tin plate and read for a while. One night for some reason I had left my plate outside and now tucked into my sleeping bag I didn't want to get out again. I lit my candle and placed it on my plastic washing kit box. Once the candle had burned down and started flickering making it impossible to read further, I fell asleep instantly. Next thing I knew the tent was full of smoke and there were flames in front of my face. The wash kit was on fire; I quickly threw it outside making sure all fire was extinguished. It was December 25th and with the time difference, I estimated my family back home would just about be sitting down for their Christmas dinner. I don't often get home sick but…

Figure 18 Desert Camping. Such Peace.

The following morning, I was able to survey the damage from the fire, I had a hole in the tent's ground sheet and one of my trainers had melted to a slightly different shape. My toothbrush now more of a horseshoe shape and impossible to reach my back teeth. The hole in the ground sheet I fixed using a plastic bag and some duct tape.

I then became aware of shouting not too far away, scrambling out of the tent five hundred meters away a young camel was being led along by a man and it was bucking and jumping around, eventually throwing a young boy off its back. The owner then began beating the camel and proceeded to tie its front legs into a kneeling position. Giving the poor beast a final punch on its nose the owner

34

and son walked off and out of sight over a dune. At least I didn't beat my bike. The poor camel was crying and trying to follow its owner. Eventually, the owner returned and untied the animal who then meekly followed on behind.

A short time later a group of Bedouins came over the dunes bringing water, some sweet tea and unleavened bread for me. A lot of interest in the bike and the damaged tent but absolutely no possibility of understanding each other. But who needs language when you can smile and laugh. I had carried a Christmas card from my parents with me and now I gave it to the children, who allowed me to take a photo.

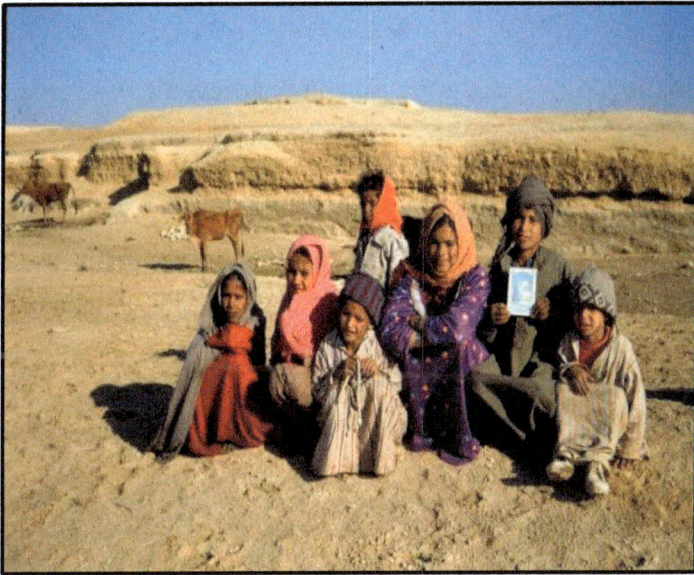

Figure 19 Christmas Day Visitors to Whom I Donated My Parents' Christmas Card.

Figure 20 The Bedouin Family Moving On.

I continued following the pipeline and eventually came across the engineer's camp, that contained about six men and little else. A smattering of English meant we got by and a pleasant evening drinking sweet tea was had. At one point I asked where the toilet was, to be told anywhere over the next ridge. They gave me a bottle of water to clean myself, which I then proceeded to make out I was going to drink, causing an uproar as they tried to stop me by graphically demonstrating how to use it, which of course I knew all along. However, this caused untold amusement and I guess toilet jokes are universal.

Eventually I could see the road ahead in the distance at which point the pipeline headed off at an angle south whereas I was to head north. No problem, I'll go straight to the road not needing the pipeline any longer for directions. The sand was once again soft and I could only drag the bike along, but I wasn't too far from the road, when I started noticing 15mm circular brass discs all around poking up through the sand. Despite the heat in the desert, I swear I went

36

icy cold and froze as I realised I was in a mine field. I didn't know what to do. Should I try to follow my tracks back to the pipeline or would I step on mines that were buried deeper. I stood there for a long time petrified, but knew I had to keep going, keeping between the uncovered mines and just hope. I tried pushing my bike in front of me but it just dug deeper into the sand. Half carrying and half dragging, desperately trying to see any of the half-buried land mines.

By reading this you'll know I made it safely. Along the road at regular distances there were signs warning not to enter because of the mines, I suspect they never thought anyone would come from over the desert. Researching for this book I read that the mines were laid down in the 1967 six-day war with Israel. It's now 2025 and the area along the road is still seen as one of the most mined areas in the world with no plan to clear them. At least I now knew which side of the road I needed to be when camping.

Returning to Gaza and into Israel I headed back to Tel Aviv and booked a flight to Bombay with an overnight stop in Rome. I could have had the overnight in London, but just the thought of going back to the UK would have felt like a failure somehow. There was so much upheaval in Africa and the Middle East that trying to get through overland was impossible.

Chapter 6: India, Nepal and almost Tibet

I have cycled twice in India and will included all the adventures in this chapter because the routes are straight forward. I had a list of places I particularly wanted to visit. From Mumbai I headed north to Rajasthan and made for Jaipur the pink city and of course the Taj Mahal in Agra. On to Delhi and heading north to cross into Nepal at Banbasa and followed the flat lowland road until turning north to Pokhara. Where I had a break from riding and took a week trekking in the Himalayans. On to Katmandu and up to the Tibetan/China border. Back to Katmandu returning to India and Boda Guya flying out of Calcutta to Thailand. My second trip took me south from Mumbai to Goa and Kerala then headed east to Mahabalipuram and back to Mumbai.

Landing in Bombay, now Mumbai, there was even more madness on the roads than in Cairo. Beware of the old London red buses, they account for "1% of the total traffic however, 2002 figures show that out of 1600 accidents, 834 were attributed to the red buses with a large number of fatalities." Hindustan Times.

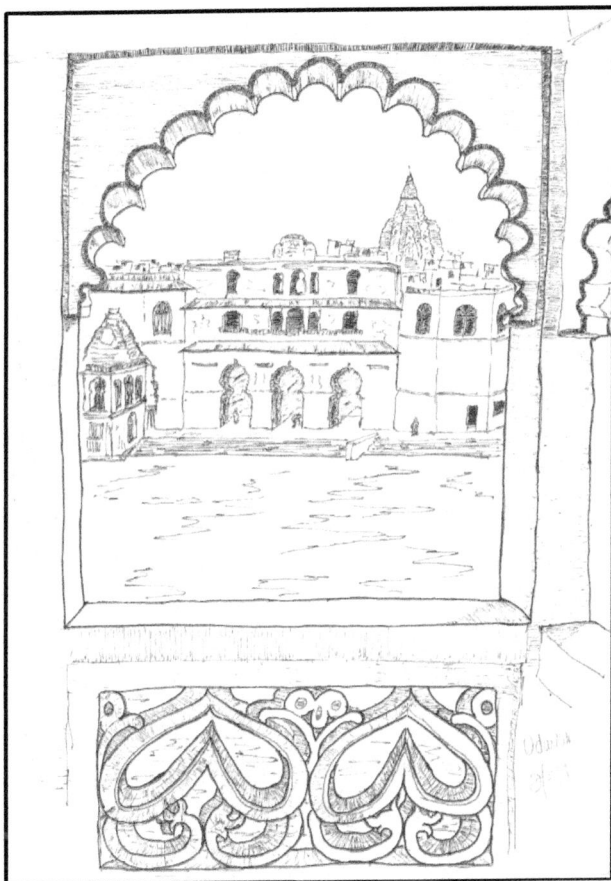

Figure 21 Hotel Room with A View.

The city is fascinating and you can always get a game of cricket on the beaches, being English everyone wanted to bowl against you, even when I was out I was allowed to remain batting to ensure everyone could have a go at taking my wicket.

The main rule of the road you need to understand is that regardless of road markings "might is right" the biggest vehicles have right of way and being on a bicycle you come bottom of the list. Away from the cities and towns you soon get to know what is coming up behind you and whether you need to get off the road. Long distance buses will have a mass of speakers on the roof playing at full volume Bollywood sound tracks with apparently the video being shown inside. Back then trucks were allowed to carry 10% above what they were registered to carry and, they all seemed to be loaded to the hilt with passengers crammed in any space available. Despite the amount of care given to the colourful art work on the trucks, maintenance took second priority.

The concerning aspect of these trucks was how they repaired split tyres. A patch from another old tyre would be bolted onto the existing tyre, meaning you can hear them coming as they clatter loudly with each revolution. The danger they posed was brought home to me one day while sitting in a roadside café, there was a massive explosion outside filling the café with dust and debris. A trucks tyre had blown and the driver decided he was not stopping to see the consequences and sped on out of the town. A local man had been standing next to the truck and it blew his face open. A table in the café was used as a stretcher to carry the man to a first aid facility. I gave these clattering trucks even more room from then on.

Police stations were a favourite place to camp, they invariably had a nice grassy area and fresh water. The main attraction being that I would get a peaceful night's sleep as it was off limits to the locals. I chose one station because I was feeling ill and needed a couple of days to rest up. The morning I was leaving, the Police Inspector gave me two warnings, first was that the hill just outside was too steep and no one had ever cycled up it and, secondly beware of the Hill Tribes who lived in the area at the top. Well of course my ridiculous male ego kicked in and I was going to make it up the hill. Why? There won't be anyone around to witness it or even care. About three quarters of the way up a bus came noisily past with

40

some young men sitting on the roof, who then proceeded to throw potatoes at me. I admit to feeling affronted thinking "don't they know I've just ridden up this mountainside that hasn't been cycled up before" Maybe I should have stayed at the Police Station a further day and fully recovered, I might not have been so grumpy. At the summit and standing all alone was one of the most beautiful women I can ever remember seeing. Dressed in a pale blue sari she waved me to stop and invited me to come to a village just off the road. How could I refuse? Just my luck she turned out to be a Catholic Nun from southern India and with several other Nuns had set up a school and clinic for the Hill Tribes. I hadn't come across the Hill Tribes prior to being warned against them by the Inspector. Suffice it to say that they were seen as lower than the lowest Caste and disliked and mistrusted by everyone. I spent a pleasant afternoon talking to the children in the school and listening to their songs and English phrases they were learning. I spent the night at the school talking to the nuns who all spoke perfect English. I declined their invitation to stay and help a visiting priest conduct a Catholic Mass at the weekend.

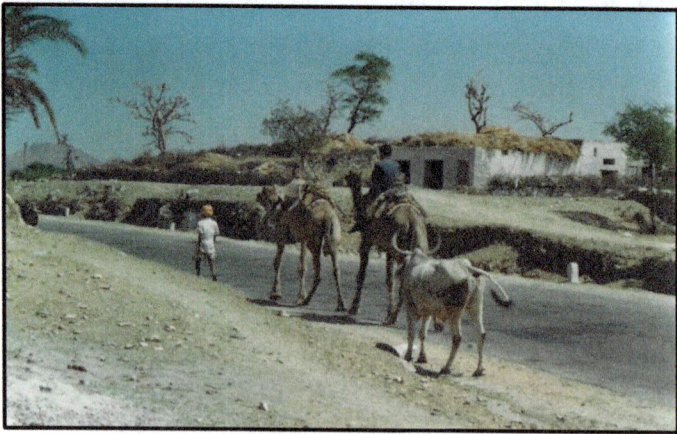

Figure 22 You Never Know Who You Might Meet Along the Road.

There were times when I couldn't avoid the main roads, however, on the plus side there were always truck stops, often made up of a large marquise with food available 24 hours. At the back would be a couple of rows of charpoys, an Indian rope woven bed you could rent by the hour to get some rest. Sleep being impossible as I found spending a night in one with the trucks coming and going all night, Bollywood music blaring out and everyone shouting over it.

Figure 23 Definitely not a charpoy in sight.

My preference was to camp but sometimes a cheap hotel was needed to get cleaned up and wash my clothes. Coming across a hostel one evening and being tired I checked in to find they only had a dormitory with twelve beds. That's ok, it wasn't the first. One thing you learn in these situations is once they see a westerner the cost is doubled. I bartered with the owner making the universal sign of cutting across your palm with your other hand to indicate I would only pay half of his asking price. He did eventually agree and I was soon in bed and, despite several other men snoring away, I was soon asleep. Shortly after, I had a rude awakening as this huge Sikh truck driver started getting into bed with me. I wasn't having this and a rumpus followed. Eventually the owner appeared and explained to me I had bargained and paid for the use of only half of the bed.

Out of the cities and tourist areas I was always seen as a curiosity, from the boy cycling past while staring intently at me until running straight into a tree, to the crowds gathering every time I stopped in a town or village. They generally had two questions, the first was how I did my ablutions, I explained the same as most people if there was a river or pond about. Leading one guy to ask "well then what is the reason you are smelling like a goat?" He clearly didn't appreciate that I had been cycling for eight hours in the heat.

Without fail I was asked, "Are you a father?" the answer is yes unless you want them staring at your groin clearly speculating as to what was wrong with you. This question came back to bite me in one village I stopped at late in the day, "Are you a father?" came the question. "Yes." I dutifully replied. My answer was met with approval and I asked if there was somewhere I could stay and I was shown to a very nice bungalow and made comfortable. My next query was if I was able to buy food somewhere. Emphatic yes replied several men shaking their heads side to side as if saying no. Shortly after that an ornate box was produced containing white leavened bread about the size of biscuits which I consumed thinking they remind me of something but couldn't recall what it was. Still hungry I decided to break out my emergency protein bars when a steaming bowl of rice and dahl arrived to my delight. Along with the meal the woman had a picture of Jesus and clearly wanted me to bless it. At this point I realised when they asked if I was a father, it was nothing to do with my ability to reproduce but they took me for a visiting priest and that's when I realised I'd eaten the holy Eucharist! Oops. All that evening I was visited by a stream of women and children, holding holy pictures for me to bless, not one to disappoint. I raked up from my memory of being brought up a

44

Catholic, the only Latin I could remember. Waving my hand in a sign of the cross muttering "Et cum spiritus" not having a clue what it meant but everyone seemed to leave happy. I ungratefully left really early in the morning in case I was expected to conduct a mass or something.

Meeting the locals was always a pleasure for me, however, sometimes it could be overwhelming and I just needed a break. On those days my plan was to ride until the light was fading fast and then dive into a field, set up my tent and enjoy the solitude. Locals, frightened of snakes when the sun goes down, always stick to the tarmacked roads so I know I won't be disturbed. Having done this and cooked my meal I settled into my sleeping bag when from the village in the distance came the sound of drumming. This continued all night, which wasn't unusual as India seems to have many celebrations and rituals that required endless drumming. I must have eventually gotten some sleep because on waking up I was aware of people milling around my tent, again nothing too unusual in that. Poking my head out I was greeted with a "Good morning" and would I like to come to the village for breakfast. I was helped to pack up my camp with the boys fighting over who was to wheel my bike back. The Indian people are always so very enthusiastic about someone "All India Touring" and very kind. After a tasty meal and general chat about my travels and their village. I asked if there had been a festival or celebration in the night. No, came the reply, they had seen my camp light and thought it was a gang planning to attack and rob the village. Explaining that drumming kept their spirits up and showed that they were not afraid. And here they were being hospitable and friendly towards me despite frightening them and making them lose a night's sleep. I was in Bihar State which back then was basically lawless with wandering gangs of robbers and killers.

"Bihar is not merely India's poorest state; it is also its most corrupt, violent and lawless state. Hundreds are reported killed here each year in scattered incidents, most of which are given little prominence in the Indian press. The dead are victims of murders or armed clashes between radical peasant militias and the police and "armies" fielded by feudal landlords." -The New York Times, 1987

The fascinating thing for me was that invites came from such an interesting array of people, one night I stayed with a cowboy, in his cow shed and, another with a living saint. I crossed into Nepal and followed the low road through the forest area. Nepal is usually seen as all mountains and home to Everest, however over 45% of the land is forest, rich with wildlife. It became a regular occurrence to come across a troop of rhesus macaque monkeys on the road and approaching them the young and females would noisily disappear off into the trees, leaving the Alfa male to defend his troop. These monkeys are renowned for their aggressiveness towards humans. There would then be a face-off between me and the boss. I have to admit when he growled and barred his green horrible teeth it did concern me that any bite might result in rabies. Usually, once he felt he had done his duty and I was across the road he could head off after the troop, a true hero.

I camped near a couple of villages on the river plain and always attracted the village children. At the time I had an ocarina and the best I could manage was, "Daisy give me your answer," but they seemed to like it, even my singing and they quickly picked up the first line. I was warned about camping there because of the rhinos who lived in the area. Just what I wanted to know before going to sleep.

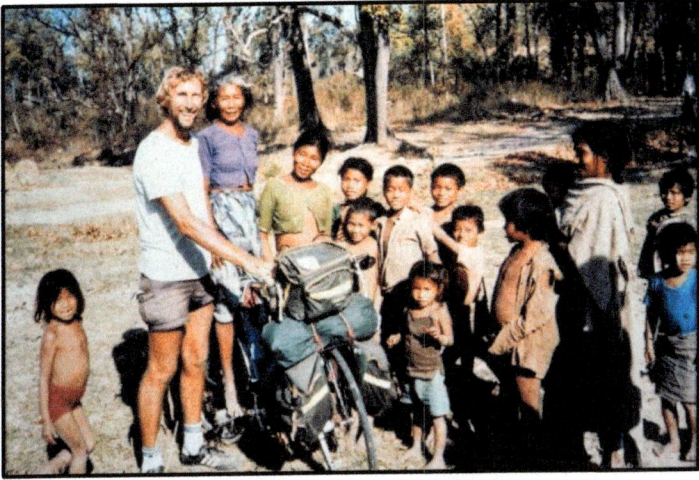

Figure 24 A Nepalese Family on the Plains.

At the next village I met one of the men who said he was a wildlife expert and guide. I agreed to hire his services and we headed into the forest. Coming across a particularly beautiful bird I asked him what kind it was. He thought for a long while and proudly announced "That is a small bird" and off we went. Now I've made some pretty awful wildlife bloops but not to his standard, like in Africa pointing out to a family two black rhinoceros and to creep up carefully keeping low, only to find it was two large boulders on the edge of the lake. A little further on he ordered me to climb up a tree quickly and sure enough a magnificent rhino appeared with her baby, she was not happy with us being around. Now I knew why my guide had been filling his pockets with stones and these he used to persuade the rhino to go away. That encounter alone was worth the money I paid him to be my guide. Several weeks later on my return journey heading for India I passed a small boy on the road side when suddenly he started singing, "Daisy... Daisy."

Heading up on one of the mountain passes in Nepal I was faced by three youths holding a long bamboo pole across the road and holding machetes. My strategy in these situations was to stop a little way off and assess what my options were, I certainly wasn't going back down and I wasn't going to go back down either. Being a fan of Biter Belker from Hill Street Blues I had long since perfected a grimace and growl. Now seemed like a good time to see how effective it was. Choosing the smallest youth, I rode as fast as I could straight at him growling out loud and one fist clenched. Just before reaching him, he dropped his end of the pole and started running and screaming as I chased him along the road. The others hadn't moved and eventually he disappeared off the side of the road leaving me to continue onto Katmandu.

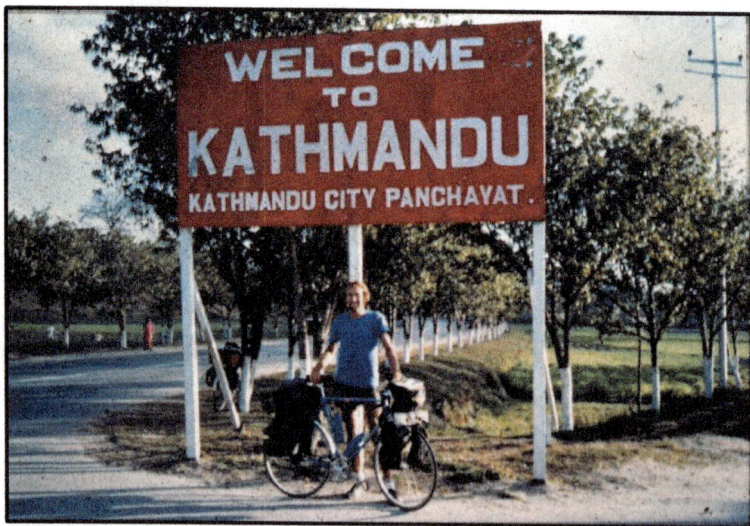

Figure 25 Entering Kathmandu

Kathmandu a fascinating city in which, my fantasy is, that at any point, you can without looking through the view finder, you can click your camera to get a most interesting shot. It is a city where a young girl is made into a living god, kept in a closed religious building with all the tourists watching the windows hoping to catch a glimpse of her.

A great place for pies based on western style food. Also, a great place to get sick with giardia as backpackers gorge on western style food, which often has not been kept or cooked correctly.

I decided to see if I could get into Tibet, despite all the troubles there with Buddhist Monks demonstrating against the Han Chinese rulers. I would take the Friendship Highway built by China linking them to India. Supposedly a trade route but cynics along the road saw it as China's route to invading India. The road surface was pretty good but you certainly knew you were in the higher reaches of the Himalayan mountains. Both the gradients and thin air made progress hard going. Getting to the border and of course it was closed and with no plans to reopen any time soon. Oh, ok, I'll just have to go back the way I came. Despite not being allowed into Tibet, I had known it was unlikely but wanted to experience the views and communities along the route. I met several ex-Gurkhas, en-route, who had bought property there. The road has since been destroyed and is impassable after the earthquakes in 2015.

Leaving Kathmandu it was mainly downhill to India, this is a two-day trip without pedalling and one hairpin bend after the other. Halfway down was a tower with accommodation at the top. The accommodation being a circular dormitory with 360-degree views across the Himalayan mountains and Everest in the distance. The place was freezing cold and on the beds were the dirtiest duvets, rivalling those you come across while trekking from Pokhara. Despite the conditions it was a brilliant place to spend the night watching the sun go down and come up the following day. There was no one else there.

The following night leaving the mountains behind I camped by a river, aware that there was a small party of local youngsters camping farther along and there to quietly party. They approached me, clearly well-educated, they respectfully asked if they could make a small mark in red on my forehead, explaining that today was the Holi Festival and colours were an important part of the day. I had no problem with this, much to their enjoyment. Crossing into India the next day, Raxaul, a typical border town, was in complete chaos as today was the Holi Festival in India and everyone was out throwing colours at each other. I thought I had avoided it by being in Nepal for the festival. However, to ensure a difference from India, Nepal has some festivals a day before India. By the time I arrived most of the men were clearly drunk and being a westerner and, on a bike, I immediately became the main target. Some were now throwing paint around and extremely boisterous. I always try to stay positive and smile but it was getting very dangerous and hard to stay upright on my bike. That was one town I was pleased to get out of. I pulled into the first truck stop where thankfully they helped me get cleaned up.

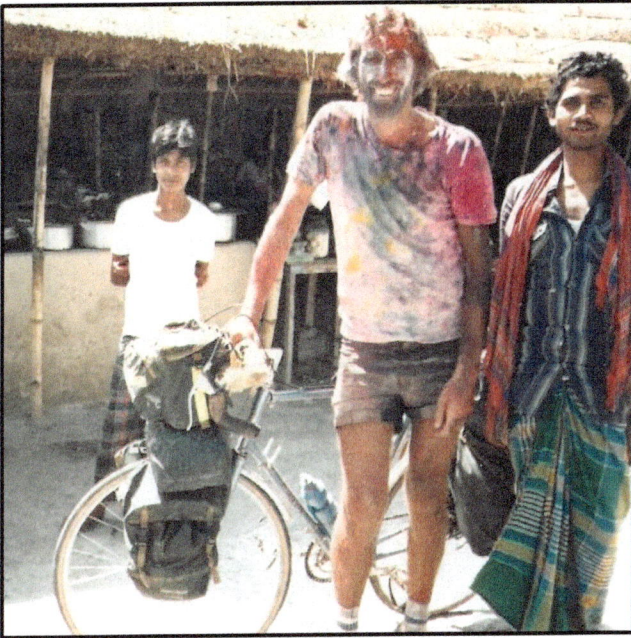

Figure 26 Aftermath of Holi Festival

While passing through a village in West Bengal, I was stopped and taken to the head man's house where he proudly told me that they were members of the Marxist "Communist Party of India". The state had a long and violent history of political turmoil. He then aggressively interrogated me about why and what I was doing there to ensure I was not a spy. Although unhappy about me being there he assured me that while I was in their village, he had a duty to ensure I was safe and looked after.

A few days later reaching the outskirts of another village I was faced with the road blocked by about twenty men clearly intent on not letting me pass. I stopped a little way back to try and assess the situation and loudly asked what the problem was. Nobody replied. This standoff lasted several minutes until a smartly dressed man came hurrying down the road and introduced himself as the Head

Man, explaining that he had passed me down the road while he was on a bus and wanted to invite me to his home for some food. As the head man he had ordered the villagers not to let me pass. That evening his wife cooked a wonderful traditional Bengal meal, Shorshe Ilish, a fish-based meal with an array of chutney that he proudly told me were award winning chutneys made by his wife. I was invited to stay the night and slept on their roof which was wonderfully cool.

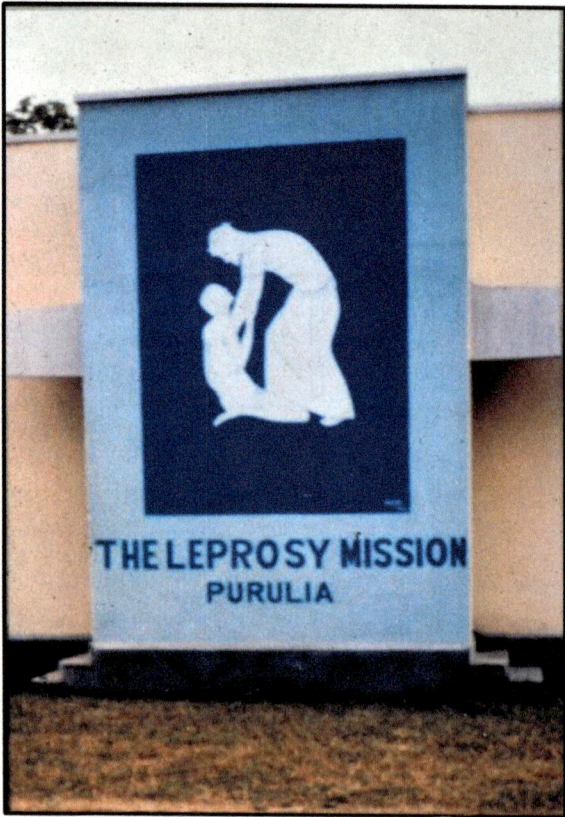

Figure 27 Leprosy Mission Barrackpore

Heading for Calcutta I came across a leprosy school and training centre in Udayan, Barrackpore and was invited to stay in a bungalow which was in the typical style of the British Raj. The head man told me that it was where the first British soldier was shot and killed during the Indian uprising. Not too sure how true this was but a good tale anyway, with this in mind and drifting off under a welcome ceiling fan, imagine my shock when a gecko fell from the ceiling and landed on my head. I stayed there several days and learnt how leprosy was perceived back then, I hope it has improved by now. I also went out with a couple of staff to the various hospitals in the area, looking at the registers for people who referred themselves with burns on a regular basis. Apparently, anyone with signs of leprosy are driven out of their homes and villages. Individuals finding signs of leprosy in the form of a sore would conceal it by burning the area. The leprosy team would try and track them down to offer them a place and treatment.

Figure 28 Leprosy Educators.

I was invited to go along with another team who would present a puppet show in an attempt to educate the villagers about leprosy and that it is treatable. On that note, an interesting aside was that some people who had leprosy would take treatment up to a certain point and stop the medication. The reason being that the states of Bihar, Mizoram and Gujarat prohibited the sale and consumption of alcohol and those with leprosy would be able to smuggle bottles of alcohol knowing the police were too afraid of contracting leprosy to ever stop and search them. This was often the only way these people could earn a living.

Later back home I was able to raise enough money to buy the colony a tractor as that is what they desperately needed. I was sad to leave this special place. Heading down the east coast I really wanted to visit the World Heritage site at Mahabalipuram and see the 7th century shrines carved out of granite on the beaches. It was also known by travellers as a great place to chill. Little did I know how the place would change my life so drastically. The hotel I stayed in was used by parties of state sponsored Russian tourists and boy how those Russians can party away from the motherland and partners' I think the women saw me as a novelty! The groups only stayed three nights before moving onto Sri Lanka and another group arrived. I became very friendly with them and was given several invites to visit the USSR. One was from a young woman, Natasha, who was later to become my wife. We will meet her again in Russia, I had no idea she was part of the Russian Mafia. Life with Natasha was like living in a B movie, that will make a book on its own.

To get a Visa to visit the then USSR you had to join Intourist, on a highly regulated official guided tour, or by individual invitations. These I started collecting and would help me to decide which route to take. Natasha lived in Leningrad, now Volgograd.

Nicholas in Ufa (that was one place I had to fly to), another Natasha in Pinsk, Belarus, and a doctor Serguei in Senno, Belarus.

Leaving Mahabalipuram and heading across the country to Kovalam in Kerala. I was cycling alongside an old Mogul wall and there on top, fast asleep in the sun was a magnificent tiger.

I quietly took a photo and was pleased to be on a quiet mode of transport. However, ahead was a narrow archway over the road and heading my way was an open back truck full of local people. Unfortunately, the driver was too close to the side and they became stuck. Everyone on board was shouting their opinion as to what the driver should do to extricate the vehicle. The noise woke the tiger, who decided to find out what all the fuss was about and walked along the wall to the archway and peered down into the truck. Understandably, this caused even more consternation and the noise level increased.

Figure 29 Apologies for the Quality of the Pic but You Can See the Truck In the Bottom Left Corner.

With that the truck shot out of the archway and sped off down the road. Thanks guys, now I have to go through the archway with a tiger prowling around on top. I waited a while and eventually the tiger disappeared into the little building on top of the archway. I had no idea now where it was. Having little option, I decided to continue on through the arch. My reasoning was that by now the tiger was either back asleep or had wandered off. Plus, if it really wanted to attack me there was no way I could out run the animal.

Chapter 7: Thailand

Since my first cycle through Thailand on my UK-Singapore trek I have been back several times to explore the country more fully. When I arrived in Bangkok from Calcutta, I was completely blown away by the wonderful bright colours from the roof tops down to the pavement. I headed to Khao San Rd, a great place to find cheap accommodation and other travellers. Not too sure where I was going, tired, hungry and choking from the exhaust pollution due to the crazy traffic, I saw a hotel and decided to check it out. Receptionist: "Ok, we have room, which girl you want?" "No, just a room please," Eventually sorted out the confusion. Hotel 15 was a brothel and all other hotels with a number are also brothels.

Onto Khao San Rd which is ideally situated for exploring Bangkok, but not by bicycle! Walking around I came across a sign for a Thai Massage, well after nine months on my bike I felt I deserved a treat. Inside there was a large area with several small cubicles made up of movable screens. Each one had a mattress on the floor and an array of oils. The place was dimly lit with soft soothing music. I was shown into one where a sign explicitly warned against any touching of the masseur. Take off your clothes, apart from your shorts I was ordered. An attractive young woman came in and began a very relaxing massage. To conclude the session, she then knelt behind me resting my head on her knees and began a head massage. By this time, I was so relaxed and close to falling asleep when suddenly she started screaming, my prosthetic eye had popped out, rolled down my cheek onto my chest, bounced on the floor and disappeared under the screen. She was in hysterics, I was still dozy and not fully realising what had happened, when two burly men rushed in shouting "not touch" "not touch" and dragging me towards the door. Before being ejected semi naked into the streets, fortunately my masseur came to her senses and managed to save me. By this time the whole place was in uproar, wanting to know what I had done. Eventually the eye was found, much to my relief. That was the first business that didn't say good bye and hoping I would visit again.

This incident took me back to 1966 when working on Fawley Power Station in the south of England on the banks of the Solent. I had a cement blow back while drilling overhead for a fixing. I made my way to the medical centre where I was laid back at an angle for the medic to wash my good eye out. I explained the other eye can be removed and I'll rinse it under the tap. But the medic insisted he could do it. At this point a young chap wandered in, he was one of the refugees saved from Tristan Da Cunha when it was evacuated due to a massive volcano eruption. The islanders had been housed in a disused RAF housing complex at Calshot. This young man had special needs and no speech. He was employed to sweep the roads around the site and would wander in and out of the facilities at will. Today it was the medical centre where he was watching as I was given an eye bath. Not surprisingly my prosthetic eye popped out and rolled down me directly towards our road sweeper, who ran out screaming, all the while the eye kept on rolling across the floor seemingly chasing the young man. He was never seen again in the medical centre.

North Thailand

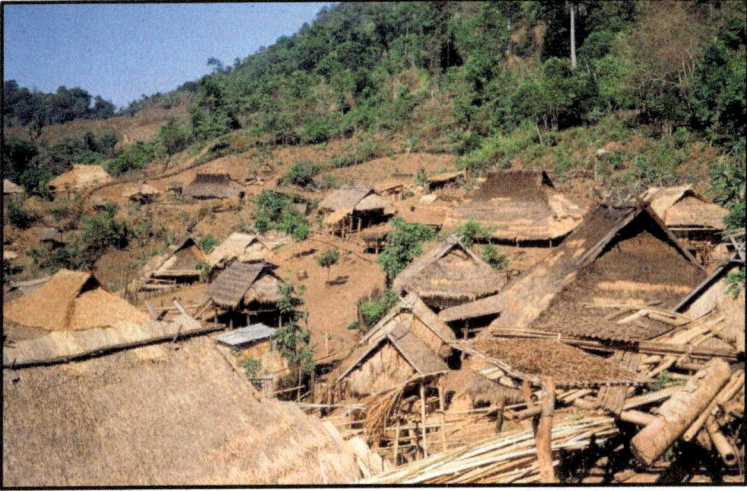

Figure 30 Hill Tribe Village Near Burmese Border

Figure 31 One of The Hill Tribe Women

Another amazing ride out of Bangkok is up north to Mae Hong Son, taking a round trip to Pai, Chiang Rai then head for the Golden

Triangle where Thailand meets Burma (Myanmar) and Laos on the Mekong River. However, there are several tracks that go up to the Burmese border, where you can cross if you want, but more likely it's where some of the minority Hill Tribes persecuted by the government seek refuge. One village I stayed in was populated by the remnants and descendants of the Emperor of China's army, driven out by Mao Zedong.

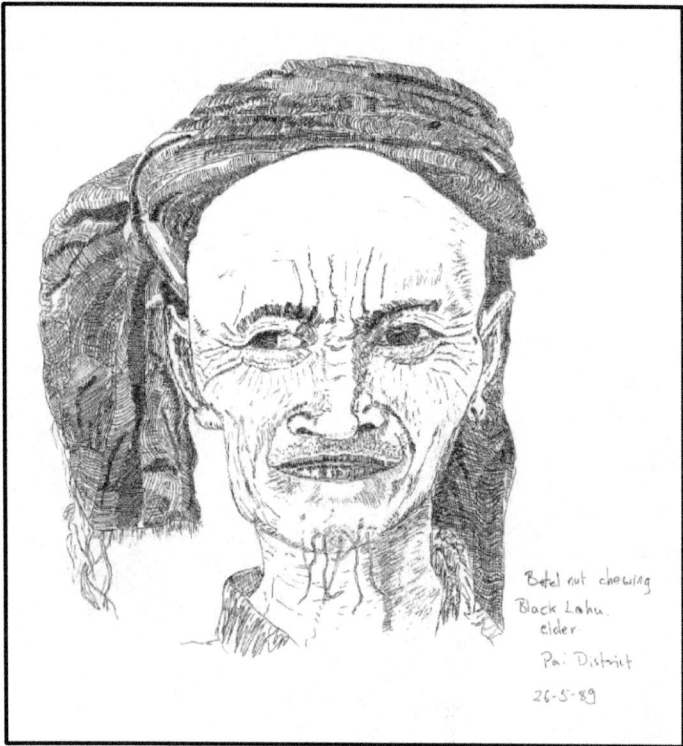

Betel nut chewing
Black Lahu
elder
Pai District
26-5-89

The security forces called Thahan Phran are recruited from prison and used outside towns where their antics cannot be seen. They wear yellow bandanas. Give them a wide berth.

23-5-89
Ban Nam Rin

Inside a Lisu Hilltribe home. This is where the food is prepared and cooked. A circular table for special occasions hangs on the wall—far right.

Figure 32 A Hill Tribe Taking Refuge from being Persecuted In Burma

Staying in Buddhist Temples overnight is a good way to discover more about the culture. Every male after 20 and before they get married are expected to at some point in their lives become a monk for a period. Boys may also spend time living in a monastery, often organised by their school.

Mostly the monks lead a peaceful life studying and practising Buddhist teachings to achieve enlightenment. They are tolerant of westerners and often keen to practice their English. I did come across a couple however, who were sitting on their "porch" happily knocking back the whiskey. Often, they may want to show you around the grounds and the different smaller shrines. One monk invited me to look around and showed me into one where you looked over into a pit, mistake, his hand came between my legs grabbing my balls firmly. They don't show you how to get out of that hold in the self-defence classes. Making it clear I was not interested, not even when enticed by the offer of a condom, he released me and we continued the tour.

Returning south to Chiang Mai where, starting to run out of time I took the train back to Bangkok.

The bridge over the River Kwai was my next destination and a ride on the Burma railroad built by the prisoners of war for the Japanese. The cemeteries are a stark reminder of the hideousness of war both on the prisoners and the local population, also enslaved to build the railway into Burma.

Figure 33 Decorating My Handlebar Bag.

Shortly after the rains came, making cycling impossible and hoping to come across a Buddhist Temple where travellers are always welcome. You can sleep in the main area providing you do not point your feet towards the statue of Buddha. The monks will share their food with you. Don't feel bad about accepting food as they have too much left over. That is why the dogs are so well fed. Early in the morning you will see a parade of monks each with a bowl for the local people to donate food, as is their duty.

With the rain teeming down I found a nunnery that willingly gave me shelter for a few nights. Every day, despite the weather I accompanied Sister Teresa, an American nun, in a battered old Tuk-Tuk as we drove around the flooded villages.

Figure 34 When It Rains...

to homes on stilts that were marooned. Our mission was to check on various vulnerable people and deliver medication. One guy needing his meds refused to walk through the water because he was frightened of snakes. Sister Teresa hauled up her habit without a second thought and waded out to his house delivering the meds. As for snakes they also didn't like the flooded ground and had made their way onto the roads, which seemed to be alive with thousands of snakes writhing around. With the rain easing I set off, but with the fields still flooded, I needed all my skills, honed back home missing pot holes, to ensure I didn't run over any snakes.

Figure 35 Tracks by Now Just About Passable.

Once the sun reappears things dry out quickly, steam coming up off the roads made for a surrealistic ride and bumpy as I could no longer see where the snakes were. At one point, thinking I must be really tired and struggling to make any progress, I realised why, the tarmac was melting and it was like cycling through treacle. To overcome this, I set off before sunrise and found somewhere for the night when it got too sticky.

All the way down to the Malay border is a cyclist dream following the coast road with camping on the beach and small hotels. Just before Tesaban Tha Thong I found a nice camp site next to the beach, I was all set up when two coach loads of children, aged about 9-11 years and accompanied by several teachers arrived. They had reserved the camp site, but said it was OK for me to remain. The children were great, no bad behaviour and they got on with erecting their tents, starting a fire and cooking their own meal. Of course, they were interested in me but had been told not to disturb me, however the teachers asked if the children could ask for my autograph! My puppets were a hit especially when the crocodile bit my nose

I had a nice meal with the teachers and all was very relaxed and friendly. After the children went to bed, I was left with the teachers, all young women and one very effeminate young man being very overtly camp but funny with it. They asked if I wanted to play Sepik Takraw, where we all stood round in a circle and using a rattan ball, the aim was to kick it up in the air and try not to let it hit the ground. I seemed to become a team on my own as the others where now all stood opposite me so it was my turn every other go and every kick was given a loud cheer. Eventually one of the women said, "Tony, why you not wear a bra?" I didn't think my pecs were that big. Then I cottoned on, wearing gym shorts without underwear meant with each kick the teachers all had a good view. At this point I apologised and withdrew from the game rather embarrassed, with loud shouts to continue, especially from the young guy. I camped with the group for three nights but ensured I never made the same mistake again.

There was one last adventure before crossing into Malaysia. Looking for somewhere to stay I came across a Police checkpoint standing alone in the forest just north of the border near Tak Bia. Here I met Sgt Hadji and his unit. Huge Muslim influence here due to being so close to Malaysia. Sgt Hadji made me very welcome and insisted I could spend the night in the police station which had a couple of bedrooms.

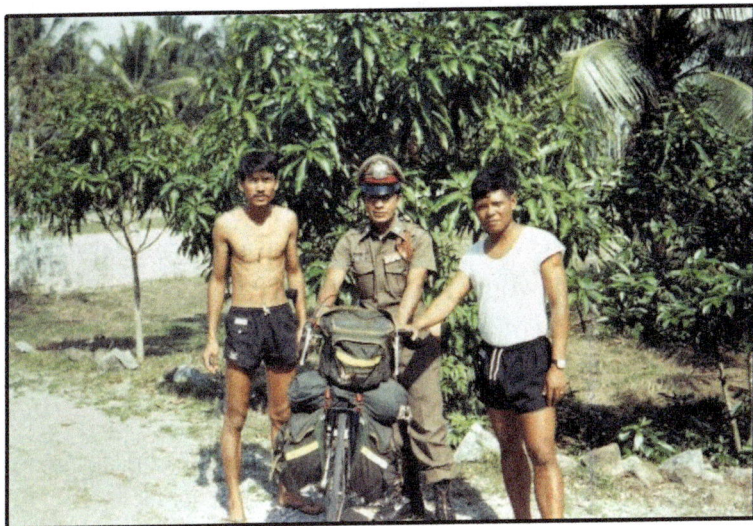

Figure 36 Sgt Hadji and Crew

Sgt Hadji, quite diminutive but confident in his authority and power, was clearly in charge. The government, in an attempt to reduce the police from being gun happy and shooting indiscriminately make them buy their own guns and ammunition. Sgt Hadji had a massive six shooter straight out of a Hollywood cowboy film and he was very proud of it. As it was Ramadan and he wanted me to join him and his family that evening for Iftar, their main meal once the sun had gone down. With me on the back of his motorbike we roared into town where I joined his wife and three children for a pleasant meal with excellent food.

After dinner Sgt Hadji announced the police and the local bank staff were having a skittles match. He was, of course, the star player. Not sure who won but with several bottles of whiskey to assist the game, it became quite raucous. Not being a big drinker, I'm not comfortable in the company of drunks. I know I'm boring. As the game concluded, Sgt Hadji announced "Now we go singsong". My plea to go to bed was dismissed under a cloud of whiskey fuelled bon-homme. Back on the motorbike we roared into the dense jungle, racing several more policemen on motorbikes, all having drunk endless amounts of whiskey. Sgt Hadji won, pumping his arm in jubilation as we arrived at a large hut, already crowded, but made welcome with a reserved long table set up with several bottles of whiskey. The only women in the place were either singing or waitressing, laughing off the groping hands that went unchallenged. I found all this hideous behaviour totally unpalatable and saying I needed to escape all the smoke, went and waited outside preferring the mosquito's company. Told you I was boring and about to get even more so.

Eventually Sgt Hadji and his men staggered out, at last we can go back and sleep. But no, Sgt Hadji proclaimed, "Now we go fucking!" Not having a clue where we were, I climbed on the motorbike again and this now drunken gang raced each other through the pitch-black jungle, Sgt Hadji won, more fist pumping. There in a clearing was an enclosure with a main building one end and several smaller units making up two other sides. Inside was little more than a scene from one of Hogarth's paintings. In tiers sat several women in what was meant to be sexy clothing. Hard to describe but I think that this was probably the end of the line for them as they looked ill and ravaged by a life of prostitution and drugs. Very young girls are often from poor farming areas and sold by their families to the brothel owners in the big cities. As they get older they are sold on to brothels in smaller towns. The police, having each chosen a girl, were heading out of the door to one of the outside units. One guy, too drunk to bother with a room, was on the floor, trousers down, having sex. On his way-out Sgt Hadji urged me to choose a girl and explained, "It's ok, you don't need to pay, we are the Police."

For me this was so wrong on so many levels. I next spent what seemed like an interminable amount of time sitting opposite the women looking at me and me looking at them, with the drunken policeman now snoring away, trousers still down round his ankles, laying on the floor between us. The race back to the police station was again won unsurprisingly by Sgt Hadji. He didn't appear the next morning and I was up and heading off to Malaysia early.

Chapter 8: Malaysia, Indonesia & Singapore

Crossing the border from Thailand into Malaysia, you immediately notice the loss of the vibrant colours associated with the Thai culture. Malaysia has four distinct ethnic groups: the Malays, who have the political power; the Chinese, who are the main business owners and have the wealth; the Indians, who tend to do the labouring jobs; and the Orang Asli, meaning Original People.

These indigenous people live a peaceful life in the jungles of Malaysia. Or rather, they did as they are constantly, like the animals, under threat of deforestation as vast areas are being cleared to make way for palm oil plantations. Many of the Orang Asli have been forcibly relocated to specially built villages.

Figure 37 Chinese Doesn't Always Translate Too Well.

I have, over several years, explored most areas in Malaysia on my bicycle and foot. Heading for Singapore along the east coast stopping off for a while on Pula Tioman, a small island used for several films notably South Pacific, because of its white beaches and clear blue sea. On the east side is the most beautiful unspoilt deserted beach imaginable. Deserted all except the sand fleas which make it intolerable to spend any time there.

One night while camping on the beach a giant leatherback turtle painfully and slowly dragged herself up the beach in order to lay her eggs. It all sounded so laboured and they have a thick oily substance to keep their eyes moist but as it slides down her face it gives the impression of crying.

Along the coast, I stayed in a couple of small beach lodges several times, such as the Coconut Lodge, which was owned by a young couple. The young woman from Europe and her husband was a local. He hand-painted T-shirts with the resort name and a coconut. Unfortunately, he has Tourette's Syndrome and sometimes while painting a tee he would suddenly exclaim out loud "Fooook" jerking at the same moment sending his loaded paint brush across the tee. These "spoilt" tees he sold for cost, but they soon became "a thing," and if you came across another traveller wearing one, you would swap tales of the Coconut Lodge. Always wondered why, when he had a tic, he invariably swore in English, not his native language.

Another one of my favourite places in Terengganu village was Awi's Yellow house, which is a series of wooden rooms built on stilts over the water. Very basic but a great sanctuary and a popular stop off for artists. Toilet arrangements need a mention, just a hole in a cubicle floor, beneath which were always several large catfish just waiting for the next meal!

Figure 38 Terengganu

Situated on an island accessible only by ferry, I met several school girls, including Awi's daughter, who remembered my puppets from a previous visit. She took Judy away and with her friends made Judy a beautiful new outfit in traditional Malay style.

Last time I was there, a major four-lane road bridge was being constructed above the island, I can only guess the effect on the tranquillity of the island. Checking on Google Earth, this is no longer a vehicle-free island, and Awi's Yellow House is closed. It never was yellow.

In the early 80's all the young Malay men had been turned into Michael Jackson clones. They are generally his size and similar skin tone and seemingly only able to move while doing the moon walk. It was like a scene from "The Walking Dead" only with MJ clones moonwalking backwards towards you.

Before our UK to Singapore trip comes to an end. There are still many other roads to explore, each with a tale. For instance, the Timur-Barat Hwy running close to the Thai border was opened to the public in 1986, before that it was a military road built to counteract the Malay Communist Party, MCP. The MCP has a fascinating history and development, changing its name and allegiances several times. During WW2 they took on the might of the British and Japanese armies and later waged guerrilla warfare against the Malay and Thai governments. They based themselves in the rainforests spanning the border and finally disbanded in 1989, revealing two Japanese men who had remained after WW2 and joined the MCP. The history of the MCP is worth researching, and there were several villages that had curfews, making travelling in the area difficult.

I cycled the Timur-Barat Hwy just after it was opened to the public, with orders that you had to complete the section between Jelli and Gerik, 125 miles before it is closed overnight. I slept on a café table in Jelli next to the guarded road block in order to start the minute it was opened. An amazing road through virgin rain forest with a warning to look out for elephants, not MCP. One hundred twenty-five miles is not the kind of distance I had ever attempted previously, and considering it crosses three mountain ranges, it pushed me to the absolute limit. There were only military outposts along the road, moving me on if I even looked like I was slowing down.

Before this road opened, I used the extremely busy East-West main artery, Kuantan to Kuala Lumpur, twice, heading north to visit Taman Negara National Park. It was while trekking here that I formed the idea to lead an expedition to climb Gunung Tahan with a group of people registered blind. It has everything, from the tactile surface of plants to the wonderful sounds of jungle life. It would offer a once-in-a-lifetime opportunity to experience an environment so different from their own. It must be the environment, as I had another idea about trying to cycle straight through the centre of Malaysia, south to north, away from roads by following the railway line known as "the Jungle Railway". We will come to that eventually. I also met a Chinese couple who were trekking and invited me to stay with them when visiting Kuala Lumpur.

Figure 39 Orang Asli Shelter

The Orang Asli people tend not to make too much contact with visitors. Stopping for a break, I suddenly felt several nuts hitting me on the head. Looking up, I saw four youths at the top of the tree, collecting the nuts and having a bit of fun at my expense. It was good-natured and they waved and laughed.

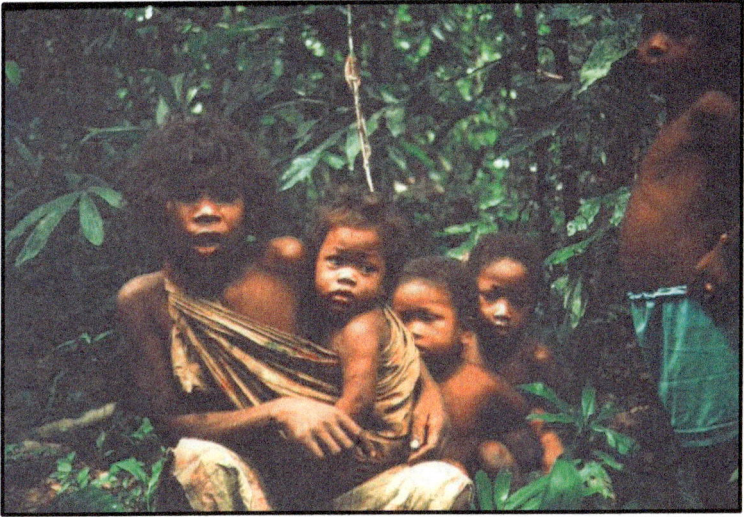

Figure 40 Orang Asli Family

The next stop is George Town on the island of Penang, which is another of my favourite places. It has wonderful, ageing British colonial architecture mixed in with Straits Chinese buildings. It also has one of the prettiest roads in the world, Jalan Kek Chuan Road. I always stayed at the New China Hotel, previously the home of Singapore founder Stamford Raffles, although he might turn in his grave if he could see it. Probably never redecorated since he left, it's now only one step up from a doss house, but a great favourite with backpackers and travellers, cheap and safe. In 1988, Chang, the owner's son, had lost money betting on the England football team in the Euro Cup, they had one game left to play against Russia, having lost all previous matches. Chang asked me what I thought the outcome would be, and I assured him there was no way England would lose all their games. So, he bet heavily to regain his losses. Russia thrashed England. After the game ended, about four in the morning, Chang burst into the packed dormitory I was sleeping in, yelling and shouting at me about how he had lost all his money. I replied, "Oh dear," and went back to sleep. He was OK in the morning, after all, he was quite used to losing at gambling.

Indonesia

Taking the ferry from George Town to Medan, North Sumatra, Indonesia and planning to do a circular tour around Lake Toba. Of all the cities I've visited, Medan was on par with New Delhi for being polluted. In their wisdom, the government banned cycle rickshaws or "becak" in the 1970s, and Medan now had the Motor Becak belching out black exhaust fumes. Apparently, the cycle Becaks caused too much traffic congestion; banning them didn't seem to have eased the congestion at all, except now you couldn't see it for the smog.

Once away from the city, North Sumatra is stunning even though it is suffering from the same deforestation for palm oil or farming that many other countries are enduring. The famous Sumatran Orangutans are critically endangered because of this and the illegal trade in hardwoods. We've been there before in both the Amazon and Malaysia.

One enduring memory I have is cycling up over a ridge and seeing below a vast basin containing Lake Toba with Toba's super-volcano in the middle, along with several other volcanoes. There are at least twelve other active volcanoes in North Sumatra. I later climbed to the rim of one, where the acrid smell of sulphur, burning your throat, means you don't hang around too long. Looking into the magma chamber, two men were collecting the sulphur known locally as "devils gold" with just a scarf as protection from the sulphurous smoke. The climb to the rim and down into the chamber was hard enough without carrying loaded baskets of sulphur rock out. This has to be up there with the most dangerous, life-shortening jobs in the world.

Circumnavigating Lake Toba was another highlight of my travels; it has everything you could wish for. Flat, quiet roads, amazing views, friendly locals and interesting places to stay. Sorry, but toilets are always an interesting, if grim, subject. Remember the ones in Awi's Yellow House with the super-sized catfish hungrily waiting for your waste? Well, here the toilets are a roofless cubicle built on stilts, with a hole in the floor. First, you need to run past a couple of large, grumpy pigs who will nudge you along depending on how hungry they are or how slow you are. It is somewhat disconcerting to look between your legs at these pigs gazing up with their mouths open. I guess this way doesn't cause sewer contamination in the lake. Maybe some of our British water companies could take note. I have wondered if maybe this is why pigs are seen as unclean and not eaten in certain religions.

There has to be a special mention for the Lake Toba Batak houses, which, with their history, design and construction, could fill a book on their own. Well worth a Google search. Remembering my personal distance record of 125 miles in one day, I set another here, only 17 miles. Just so many people to talk to and spend time looking at the art and intricacies of the Batak houses. As well as looking at the lake and volcano. Some lodges were offering free magic mushroom omelettes. Sorry, I'm too much of a coward to have tried them.

Figure 41 Batak Houses

Malaysia West Coast

Busy, densely populated, this is where commerce and shipping are mainly situated. Kuala Lumpur or KL is situated at the confluence of the Lang and Gombak rivers and means muddy estuary. Still retaining buildings from the British rule, KL is a shining modern city with 179 skyscrapers over 150m tall, with the Petronas Twin Towers being the tallest buildings in the world until 2004, but still the tallest double structure at 451.9 m. Makes my climbing the Fawley Power Station chimney at 198 m look pathetic. Amongst all this, rather incongruously sits St Mary's Cathedral, a quaint white painted church, you could mistakenly think you were in rural England. Even more bizarre, KLs wonderful railway station was built to British railway standards and can support up to 3 meters of snow! At only 3 degrees north of the equator, be sure to pack those skis.

I stayed one time with my friends from Taman Negara in north KL, very close to Batu Caves. These caves are a Hindu Temple with 272 enormously steep steps leading to a huge cave. Populated by a band of thieving Long-tailed Macaques who will swipe anything you are not hanging onto for grim life, while looking for food. There is a rumour now that they will return your camera in exchange for food. Have they really developed those bartering skills?

Figure 42 Steps into Batu Caves

The Indian labourers brought over by the British turned the cave into a Hindu shrine, dedicated to Murugan, the god of war, however, most of the Hindu deities are represented, my favourite being Hanuman the monkey god followed by Ganesha, recognised by having an elephant head.

I was there during the Thaipusam festival, where it is estimated that 1.8 million people attended over the ten days. Devotees start with a procession through KL led by a chariot containing Lord Murugan, they will then climb the steps into the cave where several ceremonies will be in progress. Many of the devotees carry a kavadi, which are a ceremonial decorated wooden structure containing milk and peacock feathers. The kavadi is very heavy and secured to their bodies by some sort of piercing or hooks, others have a spear pierced through one cheek and out of the other.

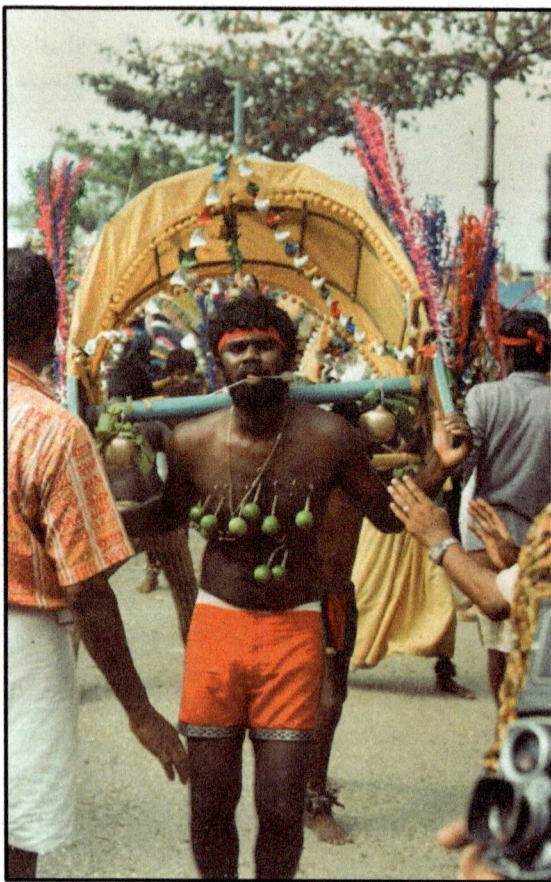

Figure 43 Thaipusam Festival

I watched this being done, and those waiting in line were just chatting away as usual, but once their turn came and the spear inserted, I never saw any blood; they would instantly go into a trance-like state and begin the climb up to the cave for Lord Murugan's blessing. All carried out to the deafening rhythm of drums and cymbals. I have an Indian friend who said that he did it one year to ask that his young son be cured of asthma. He said it wasn't instant, but his son was eventually cured.

Figure 44 A Devotee Pulling A Kavadi On Wheels.

Moving down the coast to another of my favourite towns, Malacca. Wonderful Dutch and Straits Chinese architecture abounds in this once-fought-over important port. Initially colonised by the Portuguese, taken over by the Dutch and finally by the British. Cowboy Lim, a trishaw driver, guest house owner and local medicine man, he is probably the most famous resident of Malacca, certainly among the travellers and tourists. You'll find him on most social media sites, with his famous smiling face topped by a cowboy hat. A true character. I stayed in his "Guest House" several times, where he lived with his young daughter, who insisted I entertain her with my puppets. Too many nights, Cowboy and I would visit his sister's restaurant at Gluttons Corner, where we would eat satay and

81

drink beer. Each round table had a cooking pot full of satay bubbling away inserted into the table. Lim's sister would walk between tables with a selection of small pieces of food on a wooden skewer, and you would put your choices into the pot to cook. My favourites were plantain and quail eggs. At the end of the night, your skewer collection and beer bottles are counted up; that is what you owe. Cowboy liked his beer, and when we started heading home, he would always jump in the trishaw for me to do the pedalling, much to the amusement of the other trishaw drivers.

Figure 45 Cowboy Lim, Malacca

Figure 46 Dutch Church in Malacca

Durian fruit originated in Malaysia and is best described as "looks like shit, tastes like shit and smells like shit" during the durian season it is banned from hotels, guest houses, public transport and most everywhere because of the awful smell. It does not taste too bad though; however, there are plenty of other local fruits if durian is a step too far, and mangos grow freely. I was often stopped and offered a mango straight off the tree. They would peel it and shape a "handle" to hold it. Mmmm delicious. And of course, coconuts are for sale everywhere. Before fully maturing, the green coconuts are a great, safe means of rehydrating. Often stopping in a kampung (a

village), a young boy would be dispatched to climb a coconut tree
to pick one for me.

Figure 47 Following A Track When Cycling Was Too Hard on the Railway Line

After trekking in Taman Negara, I decided to go to the Thai
border by following the Jungle Train Line, picking it up near the
compound in Jerantut, where I had left my bike before taking a boat
into Taman Negara. The tracks are laid on crushed stone, ridable but
not comfortable. I was tempted to try to hitch a ride on a train and
even decline an offer from a train driver to hop into an empty truck.
There are several small towns and villages along the route, serving
as train stops to collect the fresh bunches of the fruits taken for palm

oil extraction. The tracks are used by local people to walk from village to village. There are three wide rivers that are spanned by massive iron bridges, built by the British about a century ago. It was not easy crossing them with little room between the track and the side of the bridge; I was always in fear of a train coming. I couldn't ride across as there was nothing between the sleepers, meaning I had to carry the bike, stepping from sleeper to sleeper. I even tried rolling the bike on top of the rails, but no success. While reminding myself of town names using Google Maps, I came across photos of the bridges, now with pedestrian walkways attached, huh.

Figure 48 I Was Asked to Remove This Snake From A Family's Water Tank. I Then Made Sure They Didn't Kill It.

Entering a village, I would set up my puppet show, and within minutes, all the kids would appear along with adults. I just hoped the show matched their excitement, puppet shows in Malaysia are traditionally shadow puppets or "wayang kulit", so at least I had the novelty factor. My show was about the crocodile trying to eat the baby, and Judy fighting it off with Punch not appearing until the crocodile had gone. I only have two hands, so he couldn't help much. Regardless of how good I was, or not, it was much better than turning up somewhere and a crowd gathering, staring at me and me smiling back like a fool. I would always be welcome to sleep on someone's porch and be fed. They wouldn't accept money for food, so I gave their children a few coins to buy sweets, making me even more popular.

Figure 49 Setting Up My Show In Someone's Home.

One time, I had run out of food and came across a wooden kiosk leaning over at about 45 degrees. Hoping to find something to eat, I went to investigate, but no, he only had a few sweets. I am not a sugar-loving person, probably why the only phrase I learnt was "Tampa gula", no sugar. But I still bought half his stock, a bit mean as I'm sure there would be some disappointed children on the way home from school. I reached Kota Baru, thinking I'll not do that route again.

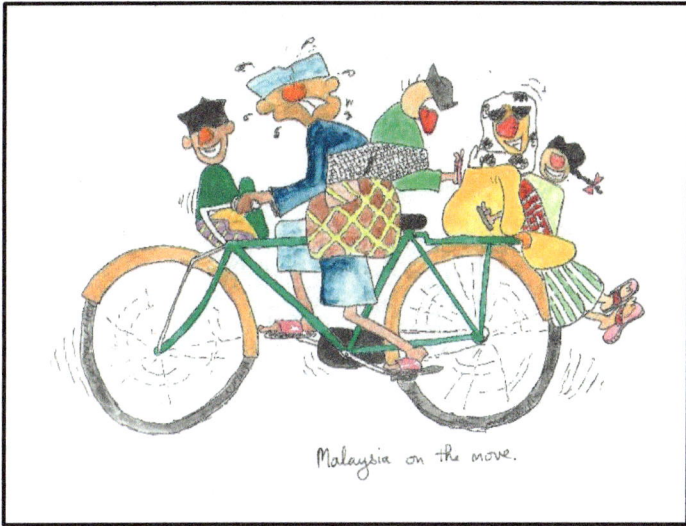

Figure 50 Bicycles Are Used to Transport Children to School.

Singapore

This high tech super commercial city with one of the world's most amazing airports at Changi. My Uncle Pat was a prisoner of war in Changi and in his notes, he tells how they would be made to manufacture boots for their captors. They would purposely leave stitching broken or loose to ensure the boots fell apart after a short while.

Singapore is a shopper's delight. I just don't do shopping, so I searched for old Singapore, with welcoming Hindu Temples and

Buddhist Shrines. Scratch the surface of this modern city, and you'll find that all the old superstitions and beliefs still abound. There is always something unexpected to experience, like being welcomed to join in a Hindu wedding or watching a Chinese Opera. Not understanding what was going on, I asked a Chinese gentleman, who told me that no one knew what was going on as it was all in ancient Chinese. This meant I could just enjoy the spectacle like everyone else. Another time, I came across an Indian youth who was apparently a living saint. Unlike the ones I had met in India, who were all much older and semi-naked. This saint was doing an elaborate dance-type routine, wielding a machete. After a while, he stuck his tongue out and ran the knife over it, causing a cut and filling his mouth with blood. People then lined up to ask him to help with a sick relative, often a child. Sticking a quill in his mouth he would write some text in his blood, which would be placed under the patient's pillow that night, in an effort to cure them.

There was even a holy snake kept in a cage, and people paid to feed it chicks. Never did find out why. While wandering around at night, I came across some very narrow roads, or rather alleyways, with booths on either side and women of all ages offering themselves for sex. Great place for food, though served on banana leaves. I was even given a masterclass in making roti.

Chapter 9: "Worse Things Happen At Sea"

Time for a break off the bike and take to the water and decide how many times does a person need to be rescued before they should give up on boats?

My first rescue was most embarrassing as it took place on the boating lake in the holiday complex of Butlins in Bogor Regis, UK. I decided to take my daughter, aged 5, for a row on the lake. Unfortunately, I hadn't realised how strong the wind was and how hopeless I was at rowing. We were instantly blown onto an island in the lake and however I tried I couldn't get away. Aware that I was becoming the focus for laughter and rude comments by other holiday guests, my daughter soon picked up on the hand gestures returning them with gusto. After an embarrassingly long time, my daughter questioned my seamanship and asked why were men moving their fists up and down? Someone eventually waded out and towed us back to the dock.

Many years later I took a boat trip to visit some smaller islands off the coast of Thailand, near Phuket, in an old wooden boat used for fishing and taking tourists for trips to the islands. Nearing one of the islands the boat lost power as the owner tried to moor up to a jetty. The waves, much rougher than normal, pushed us onto the rocks away from the jetty, where it didn't take long for the boat to break up and throw us into the water. It was a mad scramble to get onto the rocks and having lost one of my flip flops was also painful on the sharp rocky coast. Eventually everyone was safely on the jetty and the boat's owner proceeded to try and get the attention of other boats to rescue us.

The captain of another slightly larger fishing boat decided to assist us. Due to the swell he decided to anchor away from the jetty to ensure he wasn't also washed onto the rocks and slowly inch forward on his anchor rope. What happened next is a testament to how old and unsafe some of these boats are. The back half of the boat, attached to the anchor, was completely torn away and the three-man crew were forced to scramble onto the jetty. Eventually a larger fishing boat came in to rescue us all. Does that now count as four boating disasters needing to be rescued?

Phuket, now a major tourist spot, I hope there are more safety checks and licences on these tours.

1979 with a group of teenagers, who were in care, I joined Perseverance, a 36-tonne yacht, on the tall ships race starting in Oslo.

Figure 51 Getting Ready for the Off.

On leaving the safety of the Norwegian fiords the wind started getting up and we were soon in the middle of a raging storm, I remember looking up and up as wave after wave crashed down on the yacht. It was a matter of survival, apart from Dave the skipper and myself the rest of the crew were unable to come up top suffering from acute sea sickness. I'll leave you to imagine the scene down below as by now no one was making it to the heads and the floor was awash with puke. I could have coped with this until someone used my sou'wester to throw up in, very miffed and ridiculously thinking how could they, don't they know I have to go up on deck. I put it on inside out and let the elements clean it for me. By now Dave and I were doing four-hour stints on the wheel and four hours below trying to get some sleep. Did I promise you a bicycle would feature in this adventure at some point? Well, it did. By the third day I was just so exhausted and looking to my left there was an elderly woman riding alongside the yacht on a sit up and beg bicycle, complete with front basket and dressed in a white flowing dress, despite the howling wind she still managed to keep her hat on! I knew I was now hallucinating. To this day I don't remember how many days this lasted but it certainly gave me an insight into some of the conditions that family members and friends would have faced on the trawlers and seine netters that sailed out of Grimsby, my home town. The storm was followed by an eerie quiet and fog, but at last some of the others began feeling well enough to come up on deck. Dave and I had lived on chocolate bars during the storm, we were now ready for some cooked food. Even the undercooked pasta that turned up tasted good.

By now with no wind and poor visibility we were just drifting, the yacht had become unseaworthy with the engine and radio out. The bilge pump no longer worked so we had to scoop the water from the bilge and pass it up on deck. Suddenly a fog horn started wailing. Dave and I looked at each other puzzled, I went up front to see whatever I could, when out of the mist one of the North Sea Oil Drilling Platforms appeared towering above us. I yelled back that there was a "........." great rig straight ahead" Dave managed to scrape past the massive legs.

Dave had plotted our route with the aim of sighting England at the mouth of the River Thames. Using the shore line silhouette identifier and knowing we had been blown north it was with great surprise to find we were half way up the Yorkshire coast, having been blown about 200 miles north. We slowly made our way back to Southampton using only the sails. Our original plan was to complete the Tall Ships race, change the crew in Cowes and compete in the Fastnet Race.

"By the end of the *1979 Fastnet* race, 24 boats had been abandoned, five boats had sunk, 136 sailors had been rescued, and 15 sailors killed" Yachting Monthly. Circumstances and hideous weather conditions in the North Sea rendered our boat no longer seaworthy and fortunately unable to compete in the Fastnet Race.

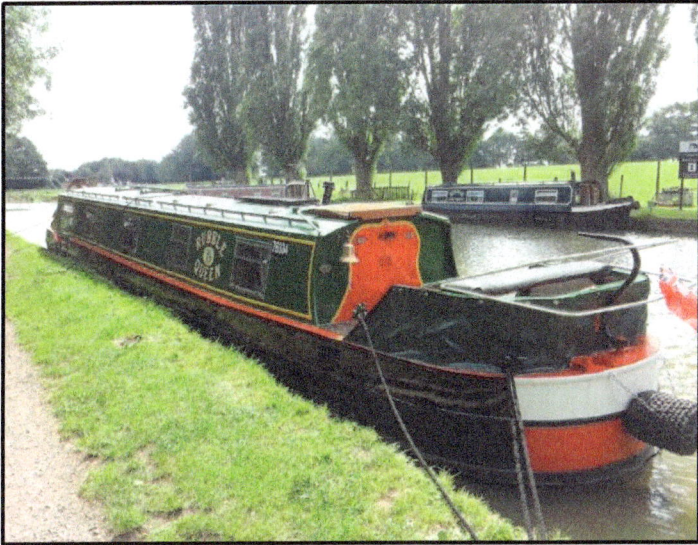

Figure 52 Rubble Queen

My next adventure on water was far more sedate and I bought a 52-foot steel narrow boat and named it "Rubble Queen" after my mother. She had been given that name by the bin men after one of them yelled down the road "Oy Fred, give us a hand the Rubble Queen's been at it again!" In the early 50's bins were carried out of your garden and manually tipped into a bin lorry; Mam never gave it a thought as to how heavy it was when filling it with old bricks and rubble.

My family and friends often joined me onboard and we shared the job of adding extra dents to the hull. The canals in England take you through beautiful countryside and the historical industrial heartland.

Once, while passing some fields I spotted a sheep in the canal, clearly in distress, with her fleece now waterlogged she was unable to get out. With my brother-in-law John (AKA Grumpy) on the tiller

I went up front and tried to lift and push the animal onto the bank. But she was too heavy. John came up front and always the hero said "I'll get in the canal," at the same time dropping his pants. The sheep took one look and with that shot out of the water onto dry land and ran. I always had my suspicions, but now it was confirmed, John had clearly been this way previously.

After several years of happily traversing the 2,000 miles of canals in the UK, with a top speed of 4mph, it all came to a dramatic end when I fell off the side of a lock into the back of the boat breaking various bones including two in my knee, I just about made it back to the marina. Despite being in pain, I didn't seek medical help for two weeks and then only because my wife, Pauline made me. While being assessed a young trainee nurse was sent over to give me the "confused old man test" because I said I couldn't remember how I came to fall off the side. "Mr. Thompson, do you know what time it is?" That was easy, "It's six minutes past eleven o'clock." she was impressed how accurate I was, I then pointed out there was a large clock on the wall behind her. Me "don't ask me what day it is because the day of the week is irrelevant to me and I never know, but I can tell you who is the King of England" Queen Elizabeth was still alive and definitely not budging off the throne. The senior nurse hearing this called a halt to the proceedings. They "booted" me up, handed me a pair of crutches and sent me on my way.

I've mentioned my voluntary work with the Blind Association. One of the favourite weekends was water sports on Hawley Lake, an MOD owned resource for learning and relaxing used by service personnel, but kindly they allowed us to use it. One of the favourite activities was rowing the "whalers" which needed six rowing and a sighted cox on the back steering. I had this idea of getting two teams and having a race. I coxed one of the boats and had six totally blind big guys in my team, all determined to win. I stood on the back and got the two boats in line. I shouted, "Ready, steady, GO!" we shot off at speed, not having sat down yet I fell off the back. No one on board realised and continued rowing as fast as possible with no cox to steer. By the time I surfaced they were too far away to hear me. They were by now getting entangled with the surfboarders and dinghy's, causing mayhem. Inevitably they came to a sudden stop when they hit the side of the lake, none of them having a clue what was going on. The life guards managed to sort them out. It took a long time for me to live that down.

Chapter 10: 1st Gunung Tahan Expedition

In the UK I was part of a group that enabled people to experience outdoor activities, Jo Diaper was the driving force being employed by Hampshire Association Care of the Blind, HACB and was keen that people expanded their activities away from the traditional tea, cake and chat.

Peter White Wicket Keeper

One of the activities was cricket with a largish ball and bells inside, the batter and fielders were good at judging where the ball was. I was asked to do a live interview on radio by Peter White a totally blind radio presenter. Peter said we will start the interview by shaking the ball and saying Tony Thompson is here to explain what that is. I said "That's Peter shaking one of his balls" the studio technicians just fell about laughing, Peter couldn't talk for laughing as for me….

Malaysia has one of the oldest rain forests on the planet, sadly under threat of illegal logging and vast areas cleared for palm oil. However, Taman Negara is a protected 4,343 sq. km parkland in the centre of Peninsula Malaysia. I first visited there in 1988 and spent two weeks trekking with a guide visiting a couple of hides that had been built next to salt licks. An amazing number of animals would come in at night for a chemical essential to their wellbeing. We spotted mainly deer and water buffalo but my favourite was watching a tapir. Unfortunately, my next sight of a tapir was it being hacked to pieces on the road clearly driven out of its territory by land clearance.

As mentioned previously I was a volunteer for HACB, doing outdoor pursuits. Jo Diaper, HACB local Chairperson, was always positive about giving people the most varied experiences possible and she was instrumental in setting up the outdoor activities, which back then was not something people with disabilities did! When I returned to the UK, I discussed the feasibility of taking a group of people with sight impairments trekking in Taman Negara. We looked at what people might gain from such an adventure apart from the physical challenge but the smells and noises alone would be wonderful. Add to that the physical challenge, the heat, the pestering insects and my cooking. How could we not get any interest? A surprising number of folks applied and after an interview on Radio Solent we also attracted a number of volunteers to act as guides. Training sessions were arranged in various national parks although none would totally get them ready for the challenge on offer. Along with this there was a lot of fund raising to be done and equipment to buy. Over the weeks slowly people dropped out for their own reasons and we were soon down to the number of people that would be workable. There would be two expeditions, the first with three partially sighted people and the second with two totally blind men. What was missing was someone with a medical background either a doctor or a nurse with possibly A&E experience. At this time in my working life, I was employed as a social worker in Southampton General Hospital and being advertised was a slide show presented by a nurse who had just returned from an expedition with Operation Raleigh. Meet the intrepid nurse Alison Farmer who I don't think thought twice about joining us.

We flew into Singapore where the heat was intense, that was enough for the members to understand this was going to be something way out of their comfort zone. With a few days for people to become more acclimatised to the heat and humidity we then took the overnight Jungle Train up the centre of Malaysia to Jerantut on the Pahang River. A two-hour boat ride took us to Taman Negaras' Park entrance, where we met our guide, Jamal, and signed in with the park officials. The first three days were fairly straight forward trekking and we made good time once we had got into our routine, with two guides to each visually impaired member. We had started to climb and while following a narrow ridge, Alan, who has a sight impairment, started to act strangely, clearly in distress. I ended up having to wrestle him to the ground to stop him going over the side. At the time we thought it was the heat, so we set up a relay of the crew climbing down to the river and bringing up water to try and get his temperature down. Eventually using two branches and my hammock we jury rigged a stretcher and carried him down to where we made the next camp. After a couple of days, we decided to leave Alan with the nurse and two of the guides, while the rest of us would make an attempt at reaching the summit of Gunung Tahan. The first day out leaving some expedition members behind in a safe camping area was weighing heavy on me. I knew they were safe. Those carrying on had put a lot of effort and money into getting to this point. At the end of that day, I decided not to go any further but to head back to the others. One of the men who stayed with Alan, Richard (Rik) wrote to me some years *later.*

"As for the trip itself, amazing, life changing, slightly disappointing we didn't get to climb Gunung Tehan, but safety of the team members more important.
When Worzel, Alan and myself were left for the rest of you to carry on, it was actually a really good couple of days, I personally spotted plenty of wildlife, some of which I thought best not to tell my companions.
I must admit I was wondering if the Orang Asli natives were cannibals as every morning there were a few watching us, this is one of the things I didn't tell my visually impaired companions, just planned my escape route 😊*"*

Returning back to the park entrance was fairly routine and the team worked really well together. Back in Singapore we sought further medical advice for Alan and they diagnosed him as having Weil's Disease.

Gunung Tahan 2ⁿᵈ Expedition

Nurse Alison and myself were joined by another Alison, a physiotherapist and two totally blind men Ken and Terry in Singapore. Giving them a couple of days to get over the flight and acclimatise to the heat I decided to recruit two more members to the squad. We were staying in a traveller's haunt and I placed an ad on the notice board. Kieran and Anita didn't take long to agree to come with us. As with the first group we took the overnight train and arranged to hire the same guide, Jamal. To ensure Ken and Terry's wellbeing each had two of the guides with them while trekking. I was used to guiding people but not in a jungle setting and the concentration needed by both the guides and those being guided was intense. Virtually every footstep had to be described, especially while climbing. We swapped guides regularly.

Figure 53 The 2nd Expedition Team

Making good time we kept to Jamal's schedule as to where we could camp at night and find water. Food wise much of it was dried noodles and meals that just needed boiling water added. Breakfast was a bag of porridge oats mixed with dried milk and boiling water. Rather than carry all our supplies up to the summit and back again, we left a batch at each camp ready for the return journey. Jamal hung the sealed bags off a high branch ensuring they were sealed to keep ants out.

Figure 54 Ken Feeling His Way Up with Direction Called Out to Him.

Our progress was steady and to reach Gunung Tahan we had to travers several smaller mountain ranges, which at times meant I had to rig up safety ropes, including while crossing fast running rivers. The technique was, I crossed the river taking the rope with me and fastened it to a tree. Returning I sent a sighted guide over first, everyone was to attach themselves downstream of the rope using a carabiner and having their rucksack only on their downstream shoulder. So that.if they were to slip and fall, the rucksack could easily be shed and not hold anyone under the water. Everyone got across safely at each river crossing despite the rapid flowing water.

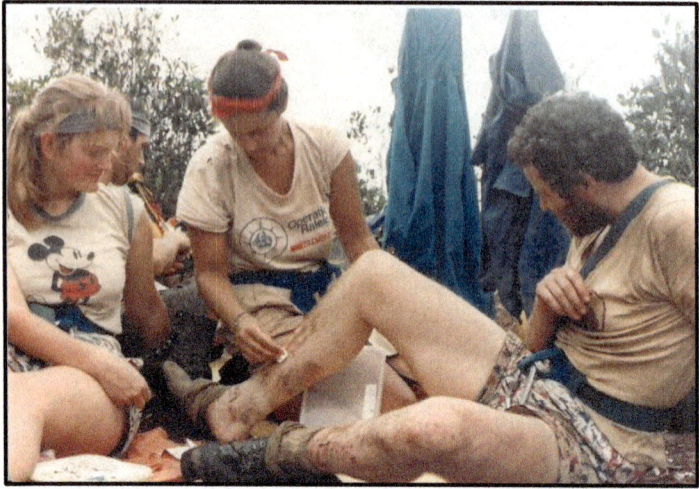
Figure 55 The Two Alisons Patching Terry Up.

Nurse Alison was kept busy having to continually patch up legs that were prone to scratches. Leaches became part of everyday life, apart from that health wise we were doing great.

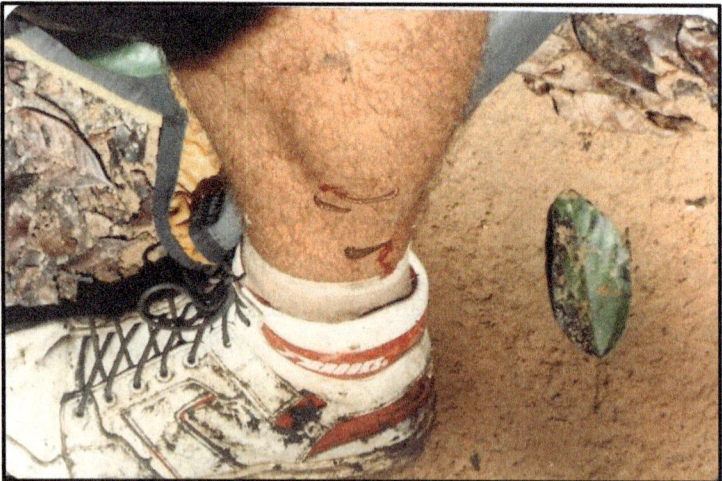
Figure 56 Leeches for Company.

Until, sitting in the larger tent at the end of the day and generally relaxing Terry felt something crawling on his leg and instinctively brushed it off. It was a centipede which landed on my leg, and ran straight up my sarong, not wearing anything under my sarong it stung me in my groin area. My god that was painful and despite my request to leave the swelling Alison gave me pain killers. The next few days trekking turned out to be very painful and uncomfortable for me.

Climbing higher we eventually got above the tree line and we were able to see more than a few feet in front of us. The dense jungle foliage was replaced by colourful shrubs and flowers such as the trumpet pitcher fly trap and wild crocuses. Making camp at the foot of the final climb to the summit we planned to head out first light, climbing and descending in one day, meaning we only had to carrying snacks and water.

That evening we discovered our camp was over-run with rats, fortunately there was the remains of a crashed plane there, enabling us to utilise its nose cone to store our food safely from the rats. The summit of Gunung Tahan was easily reached, with congratulations all round. The first time it had been climbed by blind people. The return journey seemed easier now we were in a good routine and feeling proud about having achieved the climb.

However, things in the jungle never go how you expect and, in a couple of places our food had disappeared leaving us hungry and tired. By this time everyone's clothes and footwear was beginning to rot and fall apart. A couple of us resorted to wearing one boot and one trainer.

On one particular climb, when everyone had reached the top we were unable to go further because of the fading light. Torrential rain made setting up the camp difficult but despite the difficulties and being uncomfortable I never heard anyone grumble or complain, I was so lucky to have such a brilliant expedition group. Then, when I had to climb down the ascent to collect our climbing gear, the lightning started flashing all around and I was truly worried that as soon as I reached our camp everyone would have been struck by lightning.

Two days from the park's entrance we walked into a camp to find it already occupied by a British Army Expedition. They were interested in what we were doing there, three women, four men, two of whom were totally blind and by now we were all dressed in rags. They gave a peculiar reaction to finding out we had successfully climbed Gunung Tahan. They were very sheepish and eventually admitted that they were in fact a British Army Expedition to climb Gunung Tahan, but had given up. One of the soldiers told me that earlier that day, being really hot they came across a river and all jumped in it fully clothed and had a wonderful time. Prior to flying to Malaysia, they had been deployed in Norway and were wearing temperate kit. This material soaked up the water and not having other clothes had no choice but to trek in now heavy soggy clothing, consequently they were suffering from open sores where their long trousers had been rubbing. Nothing dries in the humidity of the rain forest. It can also get surprisingly chilly if you are wet once the sun goes down.

The officer in charge didn't think they should continue as their sores would only get worse. I wish I could write that it was some other armed force than the British. They all went to bed early in their mummy sleeping bags not having tents and needing to keep their wet clothes in with them ensuring insects and scorpions couldn't take up residence. I don't think having to listen to us, still on a high, sat up enjoying talking and playing a game with sticks that Jamal had taught us did much for their mood. The rest of the trek back to the entrance went off without any further incidents. 37 years later I asked some of the expedition members what they recall, here are their answers, thank you all.

"Back in 1988, Tony decided to lead some visually-impaired people on a trek in the Malaysian rain forest, a terrain that very few V.I. People experience, with its uneven path with myriads of rocks, tree roots and branches for most of the way. Two of the totally blind members of his recruits, Ken Knowles and Terry Robinson, made it to the top of Genung Tehan, the highest peak on the Malayan mainland at 7071 feet. Among other notable memories was the deplorable break-up of the American army jungle boots they had bought specially for the trek." - Ken Knowles

"Two memorable episodes for me were the flash flood at Kuala Teku when we'd slogged along the river bank in the rain and ended up eating Crackers and Marmite for Dinner as everything was sodden, it was too late and no chance to light a fire. The water came within feet of our camp.

The second was on the way back, I think climbing Gunung Tanga Lima Belas when Lightning struck the hill we were climbing, again in torrential rain.

Of course, Tony, don't forget your intimate encounter with that centipede!" - Terry Robinson

Thanks Terry, I recall staying up all night trying to decide if we should break camp and head up higher which would mean pushing our way through dense virgin jungle in the dark. And will never forget your kindly donated centipede, thanks again.

"I met Tony co-incidentally, at the party of a friend of a friend. I told him how much I'd wanted to be part of the expedition, and he mentioned that there had been enough interest to take a second group up the mountain.

It was as simple as that.

I was then on board!

There was a training weekend arranged, but for some reason I couldn't make it, so my first experience of long distance walking, leading people who couldn't see, carrying a rucksack and experiencing tropical heat, all started on Day 1 of the expedition! The scary parts have stayed in my mind more than the brilliant parts - a rat infested camp was a real lowlight for me, the crack of a tree and a sudden deluge of water cascading down from a river we'd just crossed - we could so easily have all been swept away, was absolutely petrifying.

I also remember being very cold at night and eating the most random dehydrated foods! Although on two occasions, Ali, the nurse, produced a Mars Bar that we divided into 8 or 9 portions. It was such a morale boost. That aside, the expedition was an amazing and life affirming experience - although I was only 23, so my life wasn't really in need of any affirmation!" - Alison Taylor

Alison thanks for your contribution not only to this book but the hard work both you and Alison Farmer put into making the expedition a success.

Chapter 11: Hong Kong and China

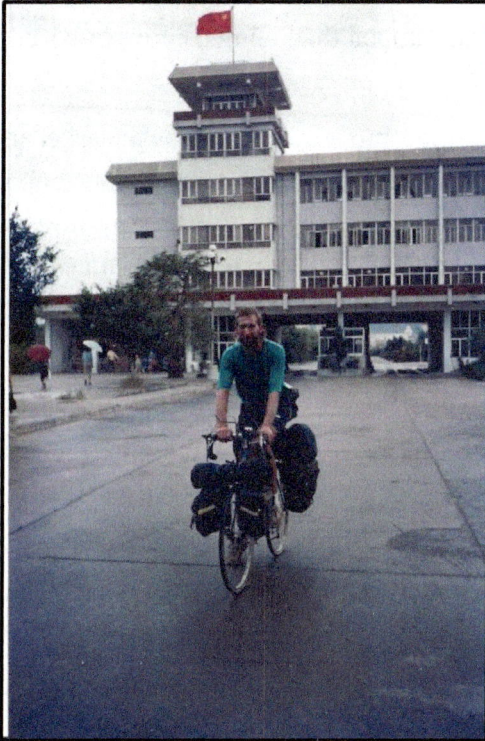

Figure 57 Chinese Border Crossing

1980s and Hong Kong was under British rule and China was still very much a peasant economy. The technical revolution hadn't taken off. You have probably worked out by now my dislike for most cities. However, Hong Kong like Rio is crazy, I loved the place.

I moved into HK's centre in a hostel next door to the notorious Chungking Mansions. It has four skyscrapers in a complex where you can find the cheapest accommodation, endless food stalls, any drugs you need and a sexual partner of your persuasion. If there is anything I have omitted, well, it'll be there. What I wanted however, was documents, maps and flashcards. They made an excellent forgery of a Taiwanese student card. China considers Taiwan to be part of China and I hoped that being a Chinese-based student would get me past any checkpoints.

You can change money on the black market in Chung King, offering some amazing rates but seeing how good they were at forgery I decided it was safer to use a bona fide money changer. There were two kinds of currency used in China, the very expensive tourist money "renminbi" and the Chinese yuan, which was illegal for non-Chinese to possess, but was a far better exchange rate.

Inspired by the pictures you see in Chinese Restaurants and Take Aways in the UK depicting ethereal scenes of tall rock formations and pagodas towering over the Li River, that was where I was going to head for, about eight hundred miles into China.

I bought two road maps, one in Chinese and the other in English, meaning I could check any road signs against the first map and then against the English version.

I found a friendly English-speaking local who wrote out several flash cards with phrases I might need.

After spending an age and a fortune at the Chinese Embassy I had my visa and was ready to go, with a warning from one of the embassy staff that only certain major cities were open to foreigners. I would be arrested and deported if I strayed outside. What gave them the idea I might, was it my cycle clips?

I was told the best border crossing for me with a bike would be through Maco. Where I found the border police all sat in a white concrete building watching TV and clearly had no intention of doing anything strenuous. I hoped they wouldn't notice my bike left just out of view, and with total boredom my passport was stamped, and after that strenuous activity, they went back to watching TV. I rode off as fast as possible waiting for a shout to stop, but nothing and I was soon able to relax.

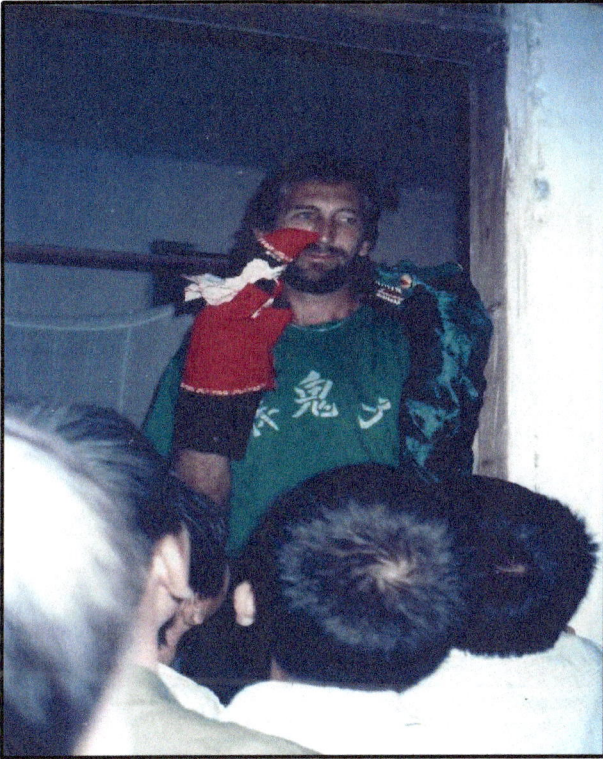

Figure 58 The Puppets Always Popular with the Children

To see China at play go to a local park on a Sunday when everyone is out dressed in their best clothes and all the local amateur entertainers set themselves up to sing, dance and perform acrobatic feats, paint etc without wanting any payment from their audience. Several times, I just sat on a bench with Punch and Judy waving at people walking by, always bringing a wave and giggle. The parks are full of colourful paper lanterns and dragons. There are permanent chess and checkers boards which attract large crowds. And if you want to gamble join in a raucous game of rock, paper, scissors. Go out early in the morning and you can join the older people doing tai chi.

Figure 59 Roads Where Mostly Hard Going

You need to understand the Chinese psyche, which is not to lose face. This can work for and against you. For instance, whenever I passed a checkpoint, the police just looked the other way rather than have to deal with a foreigner and lose face because they would be unable to speak the foreigner's language. It can also be frustrating at times trying to get a hotel room, as often I just got "Mei you" (I don't have) and walk away, regardless of whether they had a vacancy. However, if you persist, eventually a room will be found.

This backfired on me in one small town. Using my flash card which said "where is the hotel", a local pointed to a nondescript building. At the reception again I got a no. But I insisted so much that the young man on reception called for someone and a uniformed police officer came out. I was trying to check in at the Police Station. The receptionist was given the task of taking me to a lodging house.

All was fine until later that day I had a knock on the door, the receptionist now resplendent in a new police uniform three sizes too big for him and clearly wanting me to follow him back to the police station, where I was ushered into an office with a senior officer sat behind a desk who proceeded to shout at me. Next to him was an English-speaking school teacher who explained that the officer was angry because the area was closed to foreigners. It seemed to take a lot of shouting to tell me that. I produced my Taiwan student card and explained that it allowed me to travel within China and he seemed to accept that. To make matters comical the officer had his own flash card and written in English was "I am a public member" I wasn't going to disagree with that. Eventually, I was given a fine, which I paid with Chinese yuan. That set him off again, demanding to know why I didn't have tourist money. I explained -lied- that every time I paid for anything they gave me yuan in change. Phew got away with that. The officer or public member was clearly upset because with tourist money he could buy luxury western goods in special shops, usually whiskey. They explained that in the morning two policemen would come to my room and escort me to the bus station where I would be put on a bus.

111

平市县公安局

处 罚 裁 决 书

第 3 8 号

1988 年 月 日

姓名 东尼东森 男 女 41 岁 英国 籍人，

因 擅请进入不对外国人开放的地区旅行

违反 中华人民共和国外国人入境出境管理法
外国人入境出境管理法实施细则

第 46 条的规定，兹裁决

罚款伍拾元正 处罚。

局长：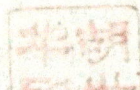

112

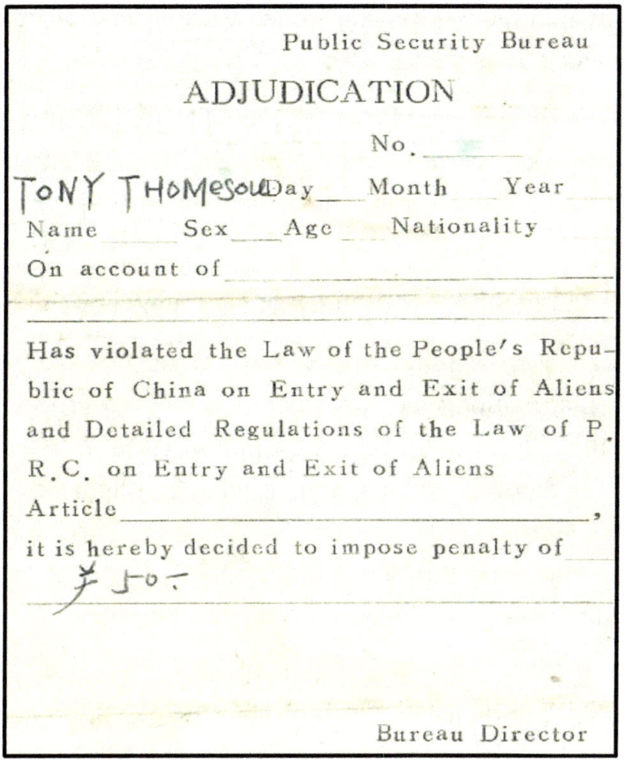

```
                        Public Security Bureau
              ADJUDICATION
                           No. _____
TONY THOMESOUDay___ Month    Year
 Name          Sex___Age___Nationality
On account of_____

_____
Has violated the Law of the People's Repu-
blic of China on Entry and Exit of Aliens
and Detailed  Regulations  of  the  Law  of  P.
R.C. on Entry and Exit of Aliens
Article_____,
it is hereby decided to impose penalty of___
     ¥50-
_____

                        Bureau Director
```

Figure 60 Having Never Even Had A Parking Ticket Back Home, I'm Now An
International Criminal. Not A Spurious Claim.

The business over, the teacher explained that the officer would like me to have dinner with him to ensure I wasn't robbed! The three of us then had a very pleasant meal paid for by the officer!

Sure enough, two young policemen turned up next morning, both now in oversized uniforms and escorted me to the bus. Waiting there was a sizable crowd, and someone who spoke English asked me to explain what was happening. He translated for the crowd and then said, "We want you to stay and be our guest." The young policemen were clearly getting concerned as the crowd began to get

113

angry at my treatment. I quickly said it was OK and I wanted to take the bus because I was tired.

As the bus accelerated away the crowd started shouting, which I took for them waving me off. But no, one of the policemen who had been securing my bike on top of the bus was still up there hanging on.

I got off at the first opportunity and continued on my bike.

The roads were mainly crushed rock, not the best for cycling and in several places along the way, there would be a group of people sitting at the side of the road with a pile of rocks in front of them and breaking them up with a hammer, when the right size, the stone would be tossed into a wheel barrow. Once the barrow was full it would be wheeled into the road, dodging between trucks and emptied out leaving the traffic to compress it down.

Finding a small hotel for the night, I had a strip wash as the water was icy cold and then headed into town for a meal. After eating I took a walk around the town and back to the hotel. Wearing flip flops, my feet needed rinsing off. One foot in the shower and bracing myself for the icy blast I turned the shower on to be scolded by boiling water. I knew I was in trouble. I couldn't make anyone in the hotel understand what had happened or where to find any medical help. Wuzhou, the next sizable town, was two days' ride away. Wrapping my foot with some bandages from my meagre first aid kit, I didn't have any choice but to ride. That was a painfully miserable two days, and I was so relieved to reach Wuzhou. It didn't take too much to spot me in a crowd and I was approached by a man who introduced himself as Mr Lie (LEE), an English teacher. He was brilliant, first helping me check in at a reasonable hotel and then flagging down a bicycle rickshaw that took us to a hospital. The

A&E room was a shock, very crowded with medics treating people in view of everyone with a pile of discarded bloody bandages in one corner. I was waved to the front of the queue and seen by an elderly doctor with the kindest eyes I have ever seen. He didn't speak English but took a lot of care removing my filthy bandage and assessing the burn. He told me, through Mr. Lie, that I didn't have an infection but he would give me antibiotics plus vitamin C tablets and not to walk too much. I returned every day to have the bandages changed. Going into the clinic I was clearly given priority ahead of the locals, which I found uncomfortable, but no one seemed to mind. I knew I would have to pay for my treatment and I was amazed when my bill amounted to pennies. Within two weeks, I was fit to ride again. During this time, I helped Mr Lie's pupils who would turn up at my room daily to talk and learn. It was good company for me and good practice for them.

It was good to be on the road again. Throughout China I met only friendly people who seemed pleased to see me. I was given a lesson in how to reap rice, and met several people who avidly listen to the BBC World Service while teaching themselves English.

Figure 61 Street Cobbler Fixing Crocodile.

One thing noticeable was the distinct lack of wildlife particularly birds. Back in the 1950s Chairman Mao ordered all sparrows to be killed as they were decimating agriculture by eating all the grain. They came up with a novel way to kill them, and that was to continually bang pans to make such a noise that eventually the birds would fall to the ground exhausted! There must have been further massacres out in the country as I never saw a bird anywhere.

Toilets, of course, need a special mention, generally communal and unbelievably smelly. One toilet consisted of a large square pit covered with a bamboo mesh which bounced as you walked on it and four holes along the centre line for you to squat over. No one ever queued so there was a mad rush whenever a vacant hole appeared, adding to the sense that the whole thing was about to collapse into the mire below. Being a westerner, I always had an audience, which was not conducive to being able to "go". Every

116

morning you would see women with a pole across their shoulders and a bucket at either end, leaving these toilets with full buckets of effluent and taking them to the fields to be used as fertiliser.

Reaching the LI River, I made Yangzhou my base and explored the local area, visiting a monastery high on a mountain top and the Stone Forest at Shillin where a local entrepreneur was charging people to ride on a zebra. No one seemed to notice it was a white horse with black stripes painted on it.

On one excursion, cycling towards me was one of the dirtiest people I have ever come across, covered in dust, and wearing a large pair of bottle bottom glasses was a young German guy. He was on a Chinese made Flying Pigeon sit up and beg bicycle. The front wheel was wobbling from side to side. He introduced himself as "Kermit", named after the puppet frog he resembled. He told me he was, in fact, registered blind but could see some things, but not up close. Hence, he had not been able to fix his wheel. I soon had the axle bearings greased up and the cones tightened. Kermit told me his father was a doctor in Germany and had given him some money to travel. Kermit had flown into Shanghai, bought the bike and had been sleeping on the side of the road for well over a 1000 km. Impressive or what? We arranged to meet up later that day in town and I told him where I was staying. Kermit had to be the coolest person I have ever met. Catching up with him later, I serviced his bike and fitted a couple of new tyres and he was ready to go. I met Kermit some months later in Thailand, he was wandering down Khao San Road in Bangkok. He said he couldn't find a room. Hardly surprising as he didn't look like he had washed since I saw him in China. I said I had a spare bed in my room which he could use but he needed to have a shower first. Kermit asked, "Do I have to wash my hair also?" You don't need to know my reply.

We eventually went our own way and sometime later I had a letter from him telling me he had had an accident in Indonesia and his glasses were too broken to wear. The poor man would be almost blind. I hope he found a friendly soul to help him. Never heard from him again.

Enjoying the view of the Li River I got talking to a Chinese man who had an amazing array of photographic equipment. He explained he was an entrepreneur with a business in Shanghai and photography was his new hobby. He hired one of the small boats that plied their trade throughout China carrying all manner of goods. I was invited to join him. Wow what an opportunity, as back then there weren't any tourist boat trips. What a magical trip I had with my new friend, who even got the boat to alter course ensuring we got all the best angles as the sun came up. Along the river were a number of fishermen standing on narrow bamboo rafts, each had several cormorants with something tied round their throats and a line on one leg. These poor birds, clearly hungry, were dropped into the water and dove down, coming back up with a fish in their beaks unable to swallow them. This was the fisherman's livelihood.

Figure 62 Monastery Up In the Mountains Survived Mao's Persecution

The area was the centre for many artists, and one elderly couple I met explained that they and their friends had been in an orchestra before Mao Zedong's cultural revolution when they had been ordered to destroy their instruments and made to work on farms. What they had done, under pain of death, was to hide the instruments in one of the monasteries up in the hills. Recently retrieving them, they planned to present an opera, now being encouraged by the new regime as a tourist attraction. I was invited to their home to watch the performance. It was a very traditional house set at one end of a walled courtyard. The orchestra was made up of several older men who said they were hoping to attract younger people to learn their instruments. I had agreed to perform my little puppet show during the interval, which seemed to go down well and made them laugh.

Figure 63 Getting Ready for the Evening Opera and Me.

All went well on my return journey to Hong Kong, taking a longer route to ensure I didn't meet my police friends again.

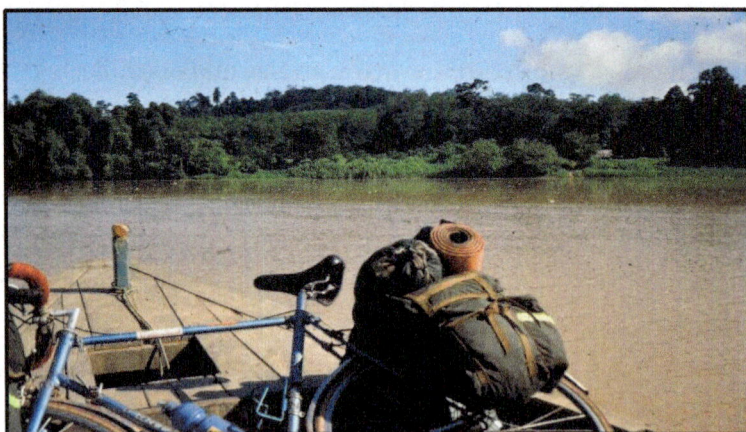

Figure 64 Ferry rowed across the rivers.

Chapter 12: USA & Canada

1987 Boston Massachusetts to Seattle mainly crossing Canada. Having spent a fabulous two weeks touring New York State and Massachusetts by car with my baby sister Diane, it was now time to get on the bike with a 3,000 mile plus ride ahead. I wanted to visit Agazzi Village, Maine, a summer camp I had worked in while doing a placement for my social work qualification.

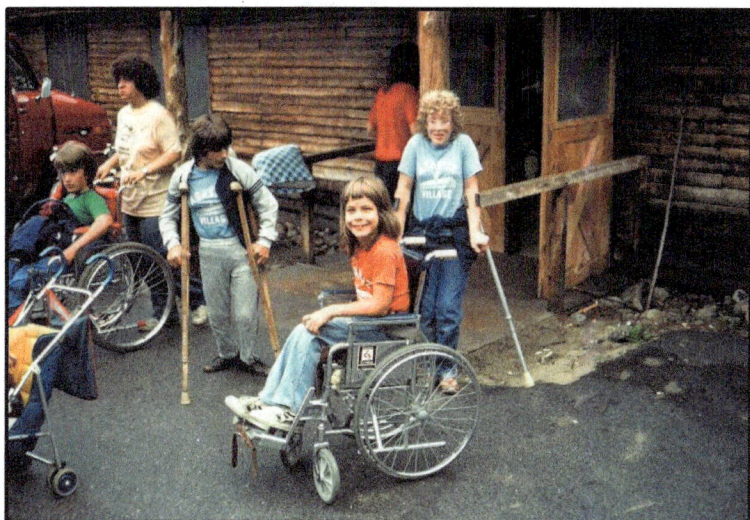

Figure 65 Agazzi Village Summer Camp.

This took me into the White Mountains and for the first and only time I almost gave up cycle touring. No-see-ums! The tiny biting midges were driving me mad, day and night they are relentless. They never bothered me while I was moving but the moment I stopped, great clouds descended on me. Looking for a place to camp I asked a local and he kindly let me put my tent up in his garden, which was enclosed in a net structure keeping the bugs at bay.

We got talking about the differences in our two countries and Brad asked if it is true that if you want to borrow something briefly you would say, "Can I pinch your……." Which I acknowledged as true. Later that evening his son, Brad Jnr, arrived and we all had a few beers. Brad Snr asked his son, "What would you say if Tony said to you, 'Can I pinch your pencil?'" Brad Jnr replied without hesitation, "I'd lay him out with one f*****g punch," Well, there's a phrase not to use outside the UK.

Dropping down from the White Mountains I enjoyed the calm easy riding of Vermont and into Montreal. From Montreal I took a side trip up to Quebec City and back. Very interesting time as I got hooked on the discussions going on around the Meech Lake Accord. I'm not sure I ever fully understood what it was about except it was something to do with changing Quebec's constitution. Quebec in places reminded me of some areas in Wales where the locals predominantly speak Welsh and often refuse to speak English to you. Having some schoolboy French I think I was treated better than the English-speaking Canadians.

I carried on down to Oka, a small town that had been in conflict, with Mohawk people protesting against the town wanting to annex part of their land to extend a golf course. A dispute that had spanned several years with violence from both sides culminating in a policeman being killed. After passing through Oka, I encountered the Mohawk people blocking the road and vehicles had to make a 100-mile detour. Must be my charm, or just looking pathetic, as I was allowed to pass unhindered, I then spent the rest of the day on virtually traffic free main roads stopping and talking to various first nation Mohawk families.

Following the Trans Canadian Highway through around 800 miles of lake and tree country, this time attacked relentlessly by bigger flies. At least you can see them. The pine forests gave way to the wheat field plains, mile after mile of never changing scenery. I treat this the same as when crossing a desert, call it cycling meditation or singing tunelessly at the top of my voice. One bonus was the prevalent westerly head winds were light.

Arriving in Calgary the annual rodeo and fair called The Calgary Stampede was in full swing. I enjoyed the country music and the general atmosphere. I have a self-imposed rule not to negatively comment on other countries' traditions and way of doing things, particularly in respect of animal welfare. I gave the rodeo a miss.

Leaving behind the plains it was such a pleasure to be climbing once again heading into the Rocky Mountains up to Banff. There are plenty of campsites and hostels on the trip to Jasper and always interesting people staying there.

Figure 66 Black Bear

Seeing animals in their natural habitat is so special and on one lonely stretch I came across a wolf standing on the opposite side of the road. I slowly stopped and we eye-balled each other for a few minutes, giving me time to take a photo before he melted into the forest. I was so excited and rode into the next camp site exclaiming to the first people I met "I've just seen a wolf" only to be met with derision and "Well we've been coming here thirty years and never seen a wolf; you probably saw a coyote." Clearly thinking that me being a foreigner would not know the difference. In Seattle I had my photographs developed and sure enough there was my magnificent wolf. How I wish we had mobile phones back then.

Figure 67 Road Cut Through A Glacier

The parks are without doubt wonderful, in fact I enjoyed them so much that when I reached Jasper I decided to turn around and cycle back to Banff. After one particularly hard day with a mile stiff climb at the end up to a hostel. I was just in sight of the place when from my left a big black bear appeared and started to walk across the road in front of me. It passed within touching distance. Dilemma! Half of me said turn round and shoot off downhill, half of me said no way you'll never get back up and half of me said get your camera out. Never was too good at fractions. Before I could decide what action to take the bear, totally ignoring me, headed off into the woods.

Next destination Vancouver where I was to stay with a couple I had met in Thailand. Fortunately, their apartment was within easy distance of Wreck Beach, the clothing optional beach. Students from the nearby university earn extra money by selling beer and various snacks including hash brownies. A great place to relax and prepare for the last section of this journey to Seattle. A combination of island hopping and ferries into Seattle and on the plane back to the UK.

Chapter 13: 12-3 USSR and Europe 1990

While in Mahabalipuram, India I stayed in the same resort as several USSR groups of tourists. I collected several names and addresses of people who invited me to visit them if I ever came to Russia. Prior to the fall of the Soviet Union there were only two ways to visit the USSR: first was through Intourist, which closely controlled and monitored your movements, and secondly, with a personal invite from a Soviet citizen. Natasha, slim, blonde and attractive, my future wife, lived in Volgograd, (previously Stalingrad) sent me an invite and after a two-hour interview at the Soviet embassy I was given a visa.

I mentioned previously that it turned out Natasha was involved with the Russian Mafia, my marriage became like a B Movie and we were divorced once it was found that Natasha was still married in Russia, this may be another book about how she was wanted by Special Branch for "piracy" and the Mafia for ripping them off. If at times it's a bit confusing, that's because Natasha's way of dealing with situations would be to "change direction". Best summed up by an English Judge during one court case at the Royal Courts of Justice, London when he said "Natasha I don't think even you know when you are lying or not"

Before leaving the UK, my sister Anne gave me an old envelope with an address written in Russian and said that this was her husband Stef's fathers' last letter from his family in Ukraine, received quite a few years ago. His father left to escape the communists. Anne asked if I could find his family, I can't imagine it would be difficult, after all the USSR isn't that big!!

Flying into Moscow I wondered if having my bicycle with me was going to be a problem, I was through within a minute.

Figure 68 Natasha

Natasha was waiting with a taxi, and we drove into Red Square and the Hotel Metropol. Security at the door scrutinised everyone and only gave access to certain people. At that point I didn't question how she managed to get a room there and had no idea that she might be part of the Russian Mafia or a business person!. Opulence doesn't begin to describe this hotel, frequented by the ruling classes of the Politburos and wealthy businessmen. The cost of a room was pennies and that evening with Natasha's friends, we ate in the hotel restaurant, unlimited black caviar, fish and chicken followed by strawberries, all washed down with four bottles of champagne. Entertainment was non-stop cabaret acts. Again, the cost was next to nothing, all grossly subsidised by the state. The hotel housed a "Beryozka shop", similar to the ones in China where you could buy western goods using Western money, preferably US dollars.

We flew to Volgograd and stayed in Natasha's flat. Volgograd lies along the banks of the River Volga. An awful place to cycle as the roads are some of the worst I had encountered, with the traffic weaving in and out and around massive potholes. I switched to the tram system as this was far quicker and safer. Apart from a tractor factory, Volgograd's only tourist attraction was the Mamayev Kurgan memorial, built to commemorate the six-month battle of Stalingrad and a Soviet victory in WW2. In the centre of Volgograd, where most of the fighting took place and kept as a memorial you can wander around the streets and what is left of the buildings.

Under the bridge crossing the Volga I met some other cyclists, or rather men with bikes. It turned out these were gay men, which was illegal then in Russia and the bicycles were their cover.

Natasha supposedly worked for Aeroflot and could organise flights for me to take a trip to Ufa, up in the Ural mountains and birth place of Rudolf Nureyev, to meet Alexei and spend a few days rafting down the River Ufa. I was surprised to see such a large population, 52% of Sunni Muslims in Ufa, restraints on religions were only just being eased. Natasha also organised for us to fly to Georgia for a holiday on the Black Sea with Artem her 4-year-old son. She also made regular flights to Singapore bringing back endless luxury goods and electronics ordered by who knows, but she didn't have any trouble bringing them back.

Returning to Volgograd I began to prepare to head home overland. Before setting out I would have to get permission to travel to the next town and repeat this at each town in order to travel onward. We visited the police station needing an official to sign my visa with the name of the next town. Even with Natasha helping me, the process took most of the day, each layer of bureaucracy requiring some kind of "gift" before being referred to the next bureaucrat. Finally, we met the main man who wrote in biro the name of the next town and scribbled his signature, not even an official stamp! Well, this was going to be easy and I certainly wasn't going to go through that rigmarole again. My route consisted of visiting some of the people I had previously met in India. Copying from my map as I progressed, I wrote in the next town and scribbled some nonsense as a signature. It was never questioned and I reached all the way and into Hungry without any problem. Well almost as you'll find out.

The cycling wasn't too difficult, but the hardest thing was finding food, shops rarely had anything on the shelves except sugar water, passing as fruit juice. What I had learnt was that most growers of fruit and vegetables sold on the black market and you had to be local to know where that was. In the villages the people where kind and would sell me fruit and bread.

I was surprised when passing the massive state-owned farms how overgrown and run down they were with ginormous farm machinery rusting away. It made wild camping easy. Many farmers are hiving off a patch of land and growing enough for their needs and selling any surplus on the black market.

My next plan was to meet Pyotr, a doctor in Orsha, Belarus. Pyotr, gave me a tour of his hospital and told me how he used to work close to Chernobyl and the awful defects of newborn babies long after the nuclear power station disaster. He was a big Beatles fan and his flat was adorned with pictures of the Fab Four. Pyotr arranged for me to stay with some friends in Minsk who were cycling enthusiasts. This was a three-day ride and I have no idea how they knew where I was, but two cyclists were waiting at the outskirts of Minsk to escort me into the city and to one of their flats. Here I got to meet a local hero who had won an Olympic gold medal for cycling in 1976, Canada. One of his thighs was the size of both of mine. He came the next day and escorted me out of Minsk to ensure I was on the correct road. For the life of me, I can't remember his name.

Figure 69 The Olympic Gold Medallist

My next stop was another Natasha who had arranged for me to stay in her friend's apartment, assuring me her husband would never attempt to visit. It turned out that Natasha worked either as or in the

130

police. I felt that it was always difficult to fully understand what people did as they seemed to be always vague. I showed her the envelope with my brother-in-law's family address on it and she said no problem as officials knew where everyone was. Sure, enough she turned up the next day with details of where they were in Ukraine. She also said that I needed to go to the police station the following day. Not

Figure 70 Cobbled Stone Roads Reminded Me of Portugal

The next day Natasha escorted me to the police station, where I was the guest of honour at a meal put on for me, as apparently, I was the first foreigner to cycle through their city. I was even given a pennant "later translated by Anastasia back in the UK as "We will achieve the victory of the Communist labour." And" A collective of Communist Labour". I have no idea what this has to do with cycling. They then loaded me up with tins of food including caviar. Natasha had tracked Steph's family down to a small village near Lviv which was close to the route I had planned. Weighed down with tins of food, my progress was slower than usual through Belarus. I stopped to buy food in one village and I left my bike locked up outside, when I came out my paniers were open and my wonderful Punch and Judy puppets had been stolen. Along with some dirty underwear used as packing. Huh.

I checked into a hostel close to the village. With eight beds to choose from, I was continually surprised at the low prices, so I decided to rent all eight beds to ensure some privacy that night and not the company of a truck driver as in India. I asked the woman at the desk where I could get a shower and she pointed to a sink behind her. By this time, I was used to odd facilities at these places and she turned her seat round to face me as I washed. I decided it wasn't going to be a strip down all over job. I won't distress you with describing the appallingly disgusting toilet down the bottom of what passed as a garden.

Cycling to the village the next day I stood outside the only shop there. Holding my sign up, that Natsha had written for me, saying" my family Frejiszyn came from this village, do you know them?" The second person got very excited and said several times "Dah, dah, dah" and rushed off. A few minutes later returning with Babushka and reading the envelope burst out crying while hugging me. She was Stephan's aunt, his father had fled the communists many years previously. A small crowd gathered and escorted me to her home with Babushka still crying and clinging to me.

132

Figure 71 Babushka Cooking

Figure 72 My Bed In the Lounge

I stayed with them for several days, woken every morning with a glass of vodka and a slice of bread. The day was taken up with her grandson escorting me to meet various people including Babushka's other brother who had written the letter, sadly seriously ill in hospital. Babushka spent her days out in a field with their two cows to ensure they were safe.

Figure 73 Babushka and Her Cows

Washing was in the river. I taught her grandson to play Frisbee, which I had with me. I felt awful when, with one throw I cut the heads off all her prize flowers destined to be used at an upcoming wedding. The wedding was to be held later that week and like everyone in the village I was invited. The problem being that by this time my clothes were getting tatty and faded in the sun. On the day of the wedding, a traditional Ukrainian shirt had been found for me with beautiful bright patterns woven into it, I was now acceptably attired. Before the service at the local church, we toasted the groom with vodka, several times.

Figure 74 Happy Couple.

All the villagers contributed to the wedding meal set out as a buffet, with vodka drunk to wash each mouthful down, or so it seemed. The day became more riotous when a four-man band started playing. Each tune being heartily toasted with vodka. This went on late into the night and before turning in for the night, babushka produced a large vodka "to help me sleep". It was sad when it came time for me to leave, just the Carpathian Mountains between the USSR and Hungary. Crossing that mountain range is quite magical, pretty villages and easy inclines, well for some of the time.

Just before the border, I met a woman who, seeing my Union flag, asked if I was English and then invited me for lunch. She lived in a nice house with her two daughters and explained that they were Hungarian and the town they lived in had been annexed from Hungary by the Soviets. As Hungarian they could cross the border without restrictions and her eldest daughter attended the university in Budapest. However, they were not allowed to sell the house and take the money into Hungry to buy another property. If they left the state would claim their property.

The border crossing was guarded by soldiers and this was the first time my visa was scrutinised, although I doubt if he knew what he was looking at. He then told me "Niet" and waved me to go back, clearly wasn't going to let me leave despite me being there illegally! Well two can play at saying "Niet" and I showed him one of my flashcards saying "Can I camp here" He became quite animated, not used to being disobeyed, and started pushing me back. Eventually in response to the shouting, an officer, who spoke some English, appeared and looking at my bike said this crossing was only for vehicles. So, I showed him my flash card again, I wasn't going anywhere. With one wave of his arm his problem was solved, the barrier lifted to allow me into Hungry. The first thing I came across was several sex shops selling material not available in the USSR.

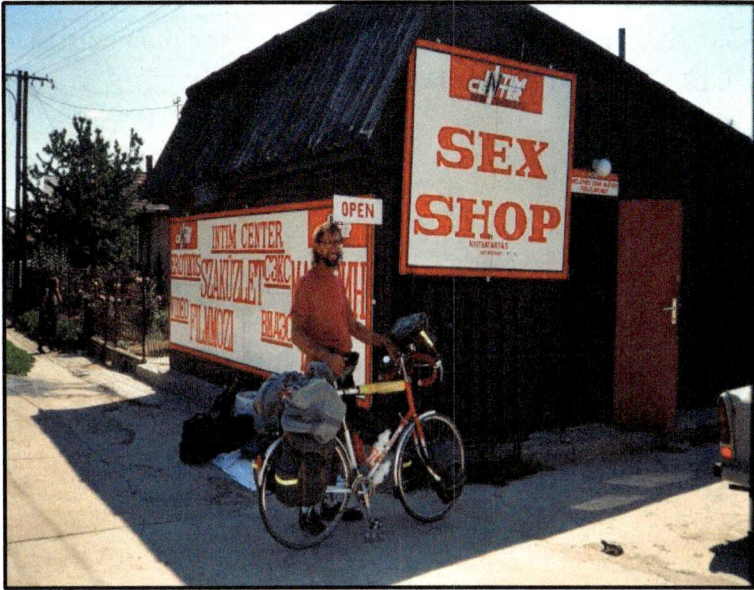

Figure 75 Just Over the Soviet Border

Europe

I have cycled in various countries in Western Europe over the years. It is just so much easier to find what you need. After the drab landscape of the USSR, it was a relief now passing field after field of sunflowers. Once in Hungary, rain became a constant, forcing me to take shelter in bars where I was invited to join in tasting the local wine. Still haven't learnt any lessons, cycling and alcohol don't readily mix.

My plan was to follow the River Danube from Budapest through Bratislava, Vienna and into Germany.

I was looking forward to a nice easy flat ride following the River Danube. Silly me. All was fine until I got into the mountain area where the Danube had broken its banks and the lowlands were flooded, forcing me to follow the river using the mountain roads. I took it as a personal affront Danube!

Chapter 14: Orlando to San Diego and North to San Francisco

Pauline (now my wife) and I owned a holiday home in Celebration, Fl. That was my starting point to cycle across the USA using the Adventure Cycling Southern Tier Route as a guide. Although I often veered from it as the mood took me.

If you ever want to see Floridian wildlife in abundance, I would suggest visiting Celebration at sun rise. Built in a conservation area the town borders mangrove swamps. I saw more wildlife in the time it took to reach the town limits than I saw for the rest of the journey. Alligators, wild boars, otters, wild turkeys, deer and a wonderful mix of wild birds.

The USA has some wonderful Rails to Trails and I built them into my route wherever possible.

I had been warned about dogs often allowed to wander freely and my first encounter was on a back road in Florida when two large white dogs came out of a property snarling and snapping at my heels. Before I could get my thoughts together a police car pulled alongside and forced the dogs away. You need luck sometimes. The officer told me that there where drug dealers in the area who had aggressive dogs specifically to keep strangers away.

I've had several encounters with dogs over the years and my strategy is to get off my bike and put it between me and the dog while shouting at it to sit. They never did but it generally brought the owner out. If all else failed, a quick squirt from my water bottle up the dogs' nose usually stopped it for long enough to make my escape. And no harm to the dog.

I followed the Coastal Highway, wild camping at night with the occasional motel to get cleaned up and laundry done. Within the usual motel chains at the cheaper end are those known as "Patel Motels" owned and run by immigrants from India. They are always good value although the towels are quite stiff and defoliate you while getting dried. Sometimes the owners can appear unfriendly, I think this is often to do with some of the racist clients they have to put up with. However, being English all I had to do was start talking about cricket, especially if there was a series being played between our two countries. I was given good service, even food at times.

Every time you check into a motel or campsite they ask if you are a member of AAA (American Automobile Association, saying you are in the AA gives the wrong impression) or another organisation. I started telling them I was a member of SOMOB and always received a discount. No one ever asked what it stood for. Were they concerned that they should know what it was or just didn't care? I decided to push my luck and tell them it stood for "Silly Old Man On a Bike" and even though I was the only member, it didn't seem to matter, I still got a discount.

St Mark's FL is a perfect little coastal town to take a couple of days' rest off the bike and get some good seafood. I met a long distant solitary hiker there, "Many Waters" who was having a few days break from walking the Florida trail and being given a bed by a now retired hiker who looks after any of the hikers who come through. Between them they had done most of the trails and Many Waters had done the Appalachian Trail, 2,190 miles, three times. The two of them reeled off several other trails like this and it was clear these hikers are tough. They all use only their Trail names- *This tradition is largely due to a combination of factors, including privacy, self-expression, and the unique culture of the trail community. Trail names help hikers feel more connected to the trail and to each other, and they can be a way of distinguishing themselves from others. AI Overview*

Stopping off in Seaside for a small bike adjustment. Everywhere was immaculate and it was where "The Trueman Show" was filmed. Not that I had heard of it until someone there told me. Hwy 98 runs along the coast with its many flat bridges which took me to Pensacola Alabama.

At Pensacola I headed inland to avoid the major cities and picked my way across Alabama. On a quiet stretch I passed four young men sitting on a bench outside a house. Nodding to acknowledge them as I passed when an empty beer can flew past my head. Why can't I just ride a bit faster and move on. But no, I had to turn around and go back. Don't get me wrong I'm not brave and have only ever got into a fight once and that was when I was about eight. Even then I was stupid, the fight was with Barry Ogden, a great lump of a boy, who later became a professional wrestler. Back to my Red Necks. Getting off my bike I walked up to them extending my arm out to shake hands. They looked puzzled but shook. I asked them what they wanted as I assumed they were trying to get my attention and maybe see if I wanted a beer on such a hot day. Sure enough a beer was produced out of a cool box and we had a pleasant thirty minute chat when I was informed they were celebrating one of them just getting out of prison. Even Mom came out and fed me fried chicken and potatoes.

I skirted to the north of Lake Pontchartrain which has the longest bridge in the world at almost 24 miles. It was very tempting to ride it and go into New Orleans but having driven there a couple of times previously I decided to give it a miss.

141

At last, I had hoped to hear it sooner, but had to wait until deep into Alabama before I got my first "Y'all have a nice day".

Picking my way across Texas on small back roads and heading for Huntsville, where I had called ahead to a bike shop and ordered a new set of tyres. Accepting a coffee, the shop owner proudly said "Look up there" pointing to a window in a bleak brick wall, "that's where we execute those on Death Row" and "if you want you can go see Ol' Sparky in the museum." I doubt if he would have been interested in my views on the death penalty and I passed on the electric chair. I needed to get some cash so went round the corner to withdraw a sizable amount. Remember back then cards were not in great use. Suddenly the bank was inundated by a bunch of men all carrying a black plastic bag and a paper chitty, detailing the amount of cash they had when jailed and what they had earned. Drawing out a large amount of cash I have to admit being slightly worried that someone might be tempted to mug me outside. I hurried back to the bike shop when the men came rushing past going towards the Greyhound bus station, I guess heading home. One young guy approached me asking desperately "Hey man do you know where McDonalds is?" Clearly been dreaming of a Big Mac while incarcerated. I felt bad, unable to help him.

Skirting round Austin Tx I stayed in a small town south of Waco. Before checking into a fairly run down hotel in the centre, I decided to cross the square and enquire at the Police Station for alternative accommodation, maybe even a night in one of their cells. There at the desk stood a Police sergeant straight out of the movies. Stocky and overweight with the mandatory bushy moustache. My enquiry came to nothing with our conversation going something like this in a Texan drawl:-

Policeman "You staying in the hotel across the road son?"

Me "yes"

Policeman "Got a gun?"

Me "No, I'm from England and if they allowed us to have guns we would probably just shoot ourselves"

Policeman "If you're staying there, you'd better git yourself a gun son"

Now I'm getting worried.

Policeman "You need a gun, cos if you don't git those roaches first, they're gonna git you." All said straight faced.

Texas took a long time to get through going via Abaline just because I like the song Abaline by George Hamilton IV. Hadn't reckoned as to how cold, wet and windy Texas could be, it was never like that on the cowboy films!

Truckers Bombs are a particular hazard I gave a wide berth to. They lurk at the side of the road waiting for an unsuspecting victim. They are plastic drink bottles, usually Coca Cola, that truckers use to pee in without the need to stop. These are then flung out of the cab and lay mouldering in the sun. Gradually they expand in the heat and eventually explode. Fortunately, I have never been the victim, but they do pose certain questions, such as the neck of the bottle is quite narrow, are American truckers particularly diminutive or just good shots? I'll leave that with you.

One trucker I met gave me a couple of free passes for truck stop showers. I only got to use one and was approached by a girl known to truckers as "lot lizards" offering her services. Even she wasn't that desperate for customers when I pointed out I was on a bicycle.

Following Interstate 20 on the service road and US-180 to Silver City, New Mexico. Birthplace of Billy the Kid. There were some bicycle races taking part including The Tour of The Gila. These you could enter as a citizen and not as a recognised race team. Huge excitement as the rumour went round that Lance Armstrong was going to enter racing for Team Mellow Johnny, his bike shop in

Austin. Armstrong was trying to get fit, after breaking his collarbone in the Tour of California, to be ready for the next Tour de France

Figure 76 Ready to Take On Lance Armstrong

Figure 77 Wait for Me Lance

Once again another of my spurious claims to fame is that I beat Lance Armstrong. Despite my coming second from last and Armstrong and Leipheimer taking the first two places. I wasn't on drugs, therefore claiming a victory over Lance. You decide.

The race had its consequences for me, a boil on my butt, giving me an enforced break and a chance to get to know the city. There were plenty of cool people around as the cycling festival continued for a further week.

Heading for Phoenix AR there are few smaller roads without taking huge detours, so I was forced to follow Interstate 10. There are often railway tracks running alongside the road and I always got a whistle blow after making an arm gesture to the drivers.

The Rio Grande River has always been a disappointment with expectation flavoured by those Cowboy films of my childhood. The

146

first time I saw it was 1977, on my first visit to the States. Camping out on Padre Island, Tx with a group of hippies, it was my turn to make the tequila run into Mexico crossing the Rio Grande at the border. I was really excited to see this famous river. Walking into Mexico from Brownsville thinking where is the river? Maybe I haven't reached it yet. I had crossed a rubbish filled ditch and was so disappointed to be told that that was the Rio Grande. I expect John Wayne would turn in his grave if he could see it now. Sorry Gen Z's, you will just have to Google him.

This trip I was due to cross it once more and even more disappointment in store as it was nothing more than a canal clearly depleted from being used to irrigate the farms.

Crossing one of the mountain ranges going from Silver City towards Phoenix I spotted a bear ahead in the shade of a tree. Not wanting to take any chances I waited a long time for a vehicle to come along going my way. Warily keeping an eye on this big animal, I waved them down and asked if they would slowly drive passed this giant of a bear and I would cycle alongside them and be shielded from it. This is how we set off and approaching the bear it became clearer that the bear had morphed into a cow's rear end. Why would a cow be up there? The car passenger sneeringly yelled out the window "it's a god-damn steer!" and sped off. Don't they know how vicious cows can be? This was not the only time I had misidentified an animal, but you will have to wait until we reach Africa in the next book.

Following the US Mexican border into California all was going well until I sprained my ankle falling off the bike while stationary, I hadn't noticed a drop to my right. Cycling was uphill as I started to cross the Rockies using the Interstate 8 (no alternative) Hot, noisy, smelly and my ankle was swelling up. I pulled off at the first junction where there was a small café and shop. I enquired about the nearest accommodation and was told that there was a complex about two miles down a track with lodges and camping. Going into reception I was met by a naked woman. They had failed to tell me it was a clothing optional establishment at the shop. I was forced to stay there until my ankle was good enough to get back on the bike and I was starting to lose my "cyclist tan".

The rest of the ride into San Diego went smoothly, taking a couple of days rest in Alpine before dropping down to San Diego. One of the few cities I came to like. I just need to head north now to meet up with my wife to be Pauline and family in San Francisco.

Enjoying some pleasant weather, nice wide shoulders keeping me away from the traffic all was good with the world. When a minivan swerved onto the hard shoulder, just about missing me and at the same time shouting loud out of the windows and blowing the horn. Startled I struggled to keep balance, wobbling uncontrollably I guess that was their aim and undoubtedly gave them a good laugh. However, just up the road the lights turned to red. Yes! Riding as fast as I could I caught them up and they still had the windows open. There was a look of horror on the driver's face and the six young men passengers all staring at me. In my best English accent, I said "Wow you can all go in the bar tonight and get free beer all night for being such heroes. When they hear you took on an old grandad who was alone on a bicycle and that there were only six of us in a minibus. You'll be pointed out in admiration as you walk about your home town." Mutterings from inside of "sorry man" and the driver desperate for the lights to change. Why didn't I leave it at that? No, I had to continue, "I'm from England and you have let your country down and let yourselves down," just how pompous can I get and I wish I hadn't said the last bit.

Once on the Californian coast road CA1, the scenery is wonderful and on one beach the seals kept me entertained while I ate my lunch. The road is narrow and popular with people renting mobile homes who are possibly not used to the width. Some just forget to fold the step into place ready to chop your leg off. Not a ride I would repeat.

Reaching San Francisco and meeting up with Pauline and family for a few days and after seeing the sights a flight home.

Chapter 15: East Coast - Celebration FL to Wilmington, North Carolina

This was a pleasant 800-mile ride, the highlight being my arrival in a small town called Andrews, SC, where they proudly announced that Chubby Checker had been born there. Now Chubby is a hero of mine because when I was fourteen and going to the local youth club, everything was rock n roll and if, like me, you couldn't jive then you became one of those sad muppets lining the wall. However, when Chubbie's record "The Twist" hit the youth culture, I could do this, giving me a chance to ask girls to dance. Thanks, Chubbie.

I met Abby the Spoon Lady busking in the centre of one of the towns. She is very talented and funny. I believe now she has quite a large following on YouTube and is doing well. I wish her all the best.

Chapter 16: LEJOG, Lands' End to John O'Groats

After having the Long-Haul Trucker touring bike specially built for me to take to Australia, I wanted to give it a really good workout to be confident nothing would let me down while in the outback, as there are few vehicles if I needed help.

Leaving Land's End in the rain I made a detour down to Marazion where I wanted to see St Michaels Mount, a small island castle that you can walk to at low tide. I have such warm memories of the place having visited several times as a child on family holidays. I arrived in the rain which was so heavy you could not even see the outline of the castle. Travelling through Devon and Cornwall I took the back roads rather than the main hideously busy A30. I have cycled across several mountain ranges but these two counties have the steepest hills one after another. At least with mountains, after climbing, you usually get a nice rest on the ride down. Not here the hills are short and steep and going down you hardly have time to catch your breath before climbing again. Plus, it was raining. I crossed Dartmoor watching the wild ponies looking as miserable as me in the rain. Stopping outside the infamous Dartmoor Prison, bleaker than I imagined, but at least the prisoners would be dry inside. I had booked into a B&B in Princetown, but the woman owner took one look at how wet I was and ordered me to strip on the porch. She brought me a bath towel and a plastic bag for my clothes. Very kindly she took my clothes and washed and dried them as well as getting me a steaming cup of hot chocolate. Ten minutes after leaving in the morning I was just as wet. I started having problems with my Achilles tendon and met up with friends Nicky and Pete near Taunton. They helped me to find a physio who

151

bound up my Achilles tendon with sticking plaster. It was OK after that, for a while. Passing just north of Bristol trying to find how to get to the Severn Bridge and cross into Wales, famous for its rain. I met a Welsh cyclist wearing a Welsh dragon cycle shirt who was going the same way. We had to put up with morons shouting, "F*** off back to your own country!" My Welsh friend actually enjoyed this and that's why he always wore that shirt. We crossed the River Severn and heading north, the road crossed the border several times with the English side flying plenty of St George flags. Oh, and it was raining. Crossing the Pennines to the Yorkshire Moors these are stunning – providing it stops raining and you could see the views. About now I started having problems with the front wheel hub. Basically, it was falling apart, stopping at a bike shop he said all you could do was replace the wheel. I was meant to meet my sister Anne and Steph locally to cycle together for a few days. They turned up in the pub I was staying at, not wet because they were in their dormobile. That's when I said enough was enough and I needed to go home as the wheel was not going to last much longer and my Achilles Tendon was starting to hurt again. Of course, not because it was still raining.

Chapter 17: Australia

2011 Perth to Adelaide, Australia – Crossing the Nullarbor Plain

Despite Bill Bryson's warning in his book "Down Under" about how Australia "has more things that will kill you than anywhere else" Fortunately, I never came across any of Bryson's killers. I only ever came across flies, mice, emus and kangaroos. Often, a kangaroo would hop alongside, keeping pace with me. I never trusted emus, though.

On the advice of a local cyclist, I took the train out of Perth to the outskirts where I was shown a brilliant traffic-free trail through the John Forrest National Park. Not until I reached Mundaring on the Great Eastern Way did I have to start mixing it with vehicles. Taking National Highway 94, traffic became lighter the further I went, mainly trucks heading for the mining area of the Gold Fields.

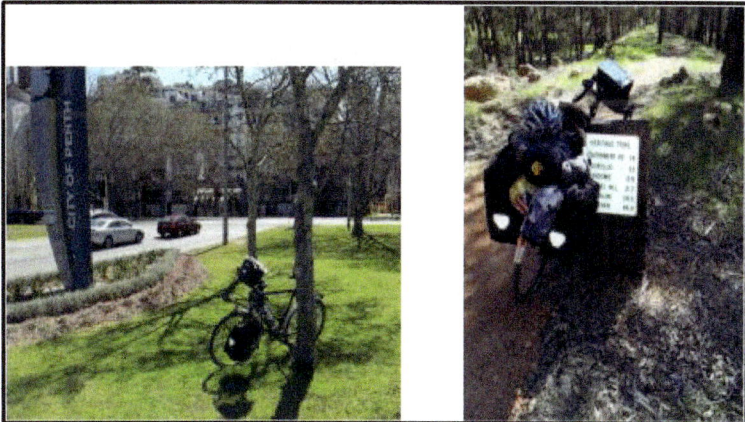

Figure 78 Perth

About 20 miles before Coolgardie, I was aware of a strange rumbling noise, sounding like an approaching train. At the time I thought I don't remember a train line running this close to the road. I was suddenly smacked in the back, my first thought was a truck had hit me, but it was a massive dust storm pushing me along, reaching speeds of 52.1 Kph registered on my bike computer. I was now going too fast to brake safely, hanging on and unable to see more than a few feet in front due to the dust and sand obscuring everything. My concern was that a truck might hit me from behind. Unable to brake fully, I had little choice but to keep going. I don't know how long this lasted, but it was over just as suddenly as it had started. Reaching Coolgardie, I found the road into town blocked by the police because so many trees were blown down and house roofs blown off. Vehicles could not get through, but thankfully, they allowed me to pass, and I came across a scene of devastation. These were people's homes, and their possessions flung around like toys. The National News Paper recorded –

"A huge dust storm tore through Kalgoorlie-Boulder yesterday as a strong cold front crossed the south of the State.
Winds of 100km/h were recorded at the Goldfields city's airport at 1.20 pm.
When the wind dropped about two hours later, Kalgoorlie-Boulder's streets had been transformed - trees were uprooted, fences had been flattened and powerlines were down. Coolgardie had several roofs ripped off during the storm and the annual Coolgardie Day Street festivities had to be abandoned." The West Australian Mon, 19 September 2011 12:43AM.

People could not believe I had survived it on a bike! I took a side trip to Kalgoorlie as I needed a new tyre, having discovered my spare – supplied and folded by the bike shop back home – would not fit. I also wanted to see the Super Pit in Kalgoorlie, 600m deep and countless other amazing stats. Peering over the side at those enormous dumper trucks looking like little matchbox toys down there. This excursion I can assure you was about a new tyre and had nothing to do with Kalgoorlie being the only town in Australia where prostitution was legal. Moving on quickly.

I reached Norseman, where one of the original gold mines is still in operation. It is the junction for the Eyre Highway, 1200 km across the Nullarbor Plain. This is what I had come for.

Crossing the Nullarbor is on most Australians' bucket list. Yet I didn't find anyone who knew how it came by its name. They all believed it was an old Aboriginal name. Nope. It's Latin for no trees, named by an Australian surveyor, E.A. Delisser. The aboriginal name is Oondin, meaning waterless. With that in mind, I loaded up 12 litres of water, dried fruit, snacks and headed out.

There are twelve Roadhouses along the highway, generally two or three days' cycling apart. They offer trucker food, rooms, and campsites. To encourage travellers to stop, they play nonstop videos of Benny Hill, who, incidentally, comes from near where we live in Eastleigh, UK.

The biggest thrill for me on long distant rides is reaching the brow of a climb and seeing a straight road disappearing into the distance. Reading about one section called the 91 mile Straight, this was worth travelling halfway around the world for. What a disappointment, yes, it is 91 miles without a curve, but it is also undulating, so you never quite get the views I was hoping for. Another oddity about the Nullarbor is it is billed as the longest golf course in the world and spans 848 miles. Each roadhouse has a hole, you bring your own clubs and balls, even I thought carrying golf clubs on my bike was one useless piece of luggage too much.

I really liked the no-frills Australian people and how they looked out for me on the road. Regularly, vehicles would pull alongside, asking if I was OK and if I needed any water.

I don't know why I was still carrying that useless tyre and as an experiment I would leave it behind in the Roadhouse café. Within an hour, a vehicle would pull alongside, and my tyre would be returned.

Out in the desert, you seem to meet interestingly different people. Peering ahead I saw what looked like a white figure walking along the road. Getting closer, I began thinking maybe I'd been in the sun too long. Up ahead was a Star Wars Trooper. Turns out he was an Ozzy doing a sponsored walk across the Nullarbor for charity. He explained that there was a team of supporters who would meet him along the route with a change of clothes and stock up his food supplies. He relied on travellers driving past for water, and they always stopped if he held up a water bottle.

One of the sad sights was cars wrapped around a post or overturned down a wash. It wasn't unusual for drivers to fall asleep due to long distances and the unchanging terrain. The massive road trains, which can reach up to 53.5 metres long, always let me know from way back they were coming up behind me and they often warned each other by radio that I was up ahead. Road trains fitted with massive bull bars needing between 100 and 200 metres to stop account for the number of dead kangaroos on the road. The drivers never attempt to stop for any animals caught in the headlight. You always know you are coming up to a dead kangaroo by the horrendous smell as it rots in the sun, giving the body a wide berth and hoping not to disturb the flies.

Australia is renowned for its flies, and I don't know who penned "Hot, Damn Hot, Flies, Damn Flies!" which just about sums it all up. Riding with a fly net over my head was essential and those March flies are like small horseflies that hunt in packs and they really know how to bite. It doesn't take long to learn the Aussie salute to waft away bush flies. While we are on about pesky things we can't ignore the mice, who constantly ran over the tent and, a couple of times managed to make a hole and get inside searching for food. That doesn't faze me. It just takes so long to get them out again.

I had hoped to see some of the feral camels left to run wild that have established themselves in the outback. Originally, they were brought over in the mid-1800s to support exploration and transport goods. Afghan men were employed as camel drivers and when the railway replaced camels it became known as the Gahn Railroad. The camels abound and cause significant ecological problems and have had a huge impact on the Aboriginal community, congregating around the traditional water holes and spoiling the water.

In an effort to control rabbits, originally brought from England to give the "gentlemen shooting sport" the government built the "rabbit proof fence" which is the longest fence in the world, 2025 miles. It didn't work.

About halfway is Eucla, this roadhouse which has its own time zone and is larger than most, used as an overnight stopping point for light aircraft doing outback tours, means there is a better menu on offer.

More importantly for me, there was a nurse-led medical centre. I had developed a boil on my butt. After three days, it was sorted, and I was ready to get back on the bike, with a bit more padding than previously.

Eucla is on the border of Western Australia and Southern Australia. While mooching around during the day, there was a tremendous roaring noise, and about a hundred bikers in convoy passed the complex accompanied by police in cars. Later that day, the police came back to the motel, and talking to them, they explained how the biker gang from Western Australia take an annual ride to meet up with a similar gang in Southern Australia to organise mutually beneficial deals. I assumed they were talking about drugs. They said that they accompanied the gang all the way to the border as they were not going to be allowed to run riot on the roads in their jurisdiction. I have never had any trouble with bikers and swapping inverted V signs when passing. Generally, they were just as interested in my travels as I was in theirs. However, there is always one!

I met the "one" just passed the border into South Australia, where they no longer had a police escort. The biker gang were on their way back and once again I had no problem until there he was, the "one", heading straight for me. Locking eyes with me. A nasty-looking sucker. Clearly intent on running me off the road. I know I'm stupid and should just let him run me off the road. But there is something in my makeup about bullies and I was not going to give way. Thinking back, that was stupid, why not let him have his sad little victory?

But I wasn't about to. Almost head-to-head, he finally pulled over, clearly angry about not winning he spat on me as he went past.

I stopped down the road to clean myself up and admit to shaking, it could have ended so badly.

My faith in people was restored that evening, camping in one of the clearings, a couple in a motorhome invited me to join them for dinner, apologising that it was only vegetables. That was absolutely fine by me. They were heading across the border the next day and there is a ban on carrying fruit and vegetables into Western Australia.

I need to mention the camping areas along the road. If you ever go that way, give them a wide berth. There is usually a single toilet structure, which is beyond disgusting if you can even get in for the flies. Most people clearly opt for the outdoors to relieve themselves meaning you have to be wary when looking for your own spot. Often, there is a water tank, drink from that at your peril, providing there is any water in it. My choice of camping was to pull off the road into the bush or camp at one of the roadhouses.

I'm a great believer in coincidence, whatever that means. One lunchtime, I stopped in a clearing with parking and one picnic table. There was already a couple there who were travelling in a Jaguar. I like to talk about Jags having owned a couple over the years. We got to talking and the woman was from England - same as me. She had been born in Grimsby – same as me. She went to St Mary's Catholic School – same as me- and knew my sisters – of course, I knew them also. They now live in Adelaide and invited me to give them a call when I arrived and go for dinner. Which I did and met their ex-Grimsby family with plenty to talk about and commiserate about when we got onto the Mariners, Grimsby's football team. Her mother knew mine, and they were in the Mothers Union together. They had a Koala Bear keep coming up to their glass house door and delightfully peering in.

The rest of the Nullarbor crossing was without incident, and I enjoyed the solitude you get only in desert areas. Eventually, the bush starts to give way to small scrubby trees and then bigger trees. Two of the trees I passed were adorned with shoes and trainers and another with bras. Can someone tell me if Australians, when travelling, carry spares in case they come across a tree that needs decorating?

I had a police car pull alongside me just for a chat. He described a small town ahead, Iron Knob, as probably the safest town in Australia. It is owned and run by a biker gang, and you do not mess with them. Iron Knob town takes its name from a hill and where the Australian iron and steel industry started, mining high-grade ore. At the time of my visit, there was no mining. However, I believe that it is about to commence again.

I didn't know what to expect heading off the main highway into Iron Knob. A pleasant tree-lined main road with typical wood framed homes. Not a motorbike to be seen. I asked the only person around and he said it was OK to camp in Knobby Park and that there was a pub that served food.

After setting up camp, I headed for the pub to be greeted by some old -timers outside who invited me to join them. It was not my lucky day. The pub didn't serve food on a Monday and there wasn't anywhere else in town that sold anything. There was only one thing left to do, buy a beer and join the guys outside. Twenty minutes later, the pub's owner came out with a steaming plate of spagbol. No charge. I liked this little town.

It was a two-day ride into Port Augusta, where I would leave the outback behind. Taking a couple of days off in Augusta, I was staying near a junction, turn right to Adelaide and my flight home or left to head up north to Coober Pedy, the opal mining centre, where people live in caves dug underground to look for opals. This place fascinated me.

Common sense eventually prevailed. With my visa running out and several other sensible reasons not to go, I reluctantly headed south towards Adelaide.

Gone now were the arid plains of the Nullarbor and, in its place, fertile farms and trees. I was enjoying a gentle ride in the spring sunshine when WACK, something hit me on the back of my helmet. All my research prior to this trip hadn't prepared me for the Swooping Season, when a variety of birds, but mainly magpies, will swoop down and hit you on the back of your head. Primarily to protect their nests. Cyclists seem to be especially targeted as they are usually moving along, this learnt behaviour clearly works for them. It is most disconcerting though, becoming a victim. This unwelcome attention followed me all the way to Adelaide.

I particularly wanted to visit the Barossa Valley, famed for its wine production and a chance to get off the main road, which was now getting very busy. Where there are farms, there are tracks and small roads. As it happened a disused rail track makes a great cycleway. I felt obliged to call in on a couple of the distilleries offering free wine tasting. I clearly hadn't learned my lesson from Romania and Hungry!

Adelaide was my final destination and my flight home.

Thanks, Australia

Figure 79 Outback Road

Chapter 18: C&O and Great Allegheny Passage plus Amish country, USA.

This was written for me by my sister Anne, who with Stef, her husband, are the only people who I have completed a trip with.

"Trip of a lifetime started with Tony planning the logistics whilst recuperating from operations and injuries in 2014. Date for trip: 11 June 2015. Bikes in boxes and they were within the weight limit of 23 kg.

The plan was to meet Tony in Washington Dulles airport. There was only ten minutes difference in time that his plane taking off at Heathrow and ours from Manchester were due to land. Tony's flight was delayed by two hours and then he was stopped by Homeland Security for a further two hours. (This happened every time due to an error made by Homeland Security four years previously!) Well, we completed the trip to Pittsburgh and back calling in Lancaster County, Gettysburg and Amish country, a total of 927 miles. Tony's skills of navigation came into their own as we cycled through Amish country. The only time we went wrong was on the second day out of Leesburg. A Highway Patrol Police man redirected us. He was stopping trucks for overweight and said Tony was ok. I said check his stomach.

On our travels we saw lots of wild life including Eagles, Buzzards, Beavers, Cardinals, Vultures, Turtles, Deer, Fire flies, Chipmunks, Black snakes, Bobcat, Muskrat, large Butterflies, but only ne Cockroach which was in Tony's bedroom. Black bears were busy chasing dogs so left us alone. And so, we joined the Chesapeake and Ohio Canal trail at Whites Ferry on the River Potomac. After riding 33 miles in temp of 38 degrees Harpers Ferry

163

will not be forgotten as Stefan had to carry our bikes and luggage up a spiral staircase (to reach a bridge over the river) *(Stef had to do all heavy lifting as I was post-surgery for another lingual hernia)*. Then we had to bike up a mountain to the hotel, not a chance of going for a beer. Tony has a sore butt and did not realise it was caused by his saddle until he bought a new one in Cumberland. A veteran cyclist with no idea!

Stunning scenery, rivers, waterfalls and trains were to feature very much on this trip. Along with all the lovely people, some strange, as we laughed all the way (well nearly). The unusual noises of the wildlife, the Cicadas' and Natter Jacks. Tony's favourite sounds the train whistles and an occasional siren certainly filled one's senses. *(Anne is referring to the fact that often our place for the night was next to a railway line and the massively long freight trains trundling past blowing their whistle to ensure I didn't leap out of bed and try to cross the line in front of them)*

People were always interested in our trip and of course Tony could not let anyone pass if they were riding an old bike. *(I collected vintage bicycles and owned about eighty)*.

Lots of rivers including the Potomac, which ran alongside the C&O canal. The river Shenandoah joined the Potomac at Harpers Ferry resulting in lots of rapids so a fantastic place for white water rafting. Tony and Stefan wouldn't come with me, so I went alone, it was great. I think the hot weather helped as it was a long trip and I got very wet. Some long tunnels the height of them was spectacular, like caverns, so tall and with a footpath as well. Very dark I think Tony was scared.

Of course, the turtles can enjoy the canals. And if one should stray then Stefan is there to help it on its way 20ft down to a raging river, oops. *(I was some way behind and finding out what they had done, especially as it was most probably a tortoise made them feel guilty)* some B&B owners pick you up from the trail as their B&Bs are right up in the mountains. Town Hill Hotel at Little Orleans was one such accommodating B&B. Every day was interesting, the B&Bs we stayed and their owners and the people we met on the trail. We met a guy called "Ray Rae" his trail name, who was walking 3000 miles. He was very wet going into Cumberland and so Tony bought him a pint of beer. He had a big bushy beard just like Liam's (their son) Some people call these walkers Hobo's.

We start the next part of our journey from Cumberland to Pittsburgh on the Great Allegheny Passage. This is a passage through the mountains originally built for the trains to move coal and steel. Scenery has changed but still spectacular as we climb to the highest point on the trail. Spent a long time watching eagles flying around the mountains, so beautiful. Over the top so should be downhill! No as the trail snakes around the mountain side, fun going down, fast as we can. Never seen Tony move so fast.

After a mega storm we had eight trees to climb over or through. *(Or rather Stef did)* we deserved a drink. No better place than at Ohioplayle where the beer is served in in jam jars. Today was a test of our stamina and yes, we must be fit. Well two of us at least.

Worried about bear! Met a lady whose Doberman dog had been frightened by a bear and ran off into the woods. Not sure if she would find him. Lots of bears in this part of the country but we didn't see any. Perhaps as well as deer's jumping out in front of us as bad enough. No animals were killed or harmed during this trip apart from a turtle (tortoise according to Tony) Stef tried to save.

165

Some random points/facts, why did Tony need a shower cap? I found 4 baseball caps. Tony renamed Maple Syrup as Waffle Juice (in my defense I occasionally lose words and have to describe them) Tony lost his wallet only once. I lost a water bottle and then found it on the way back. No beer most days.

Best joke, going through York a black man stopped us and asked why black people are tall? Pointing to his knees said "because negroes" Thought he was going to shoot us, so it was a great joke and we laughed.

As we made our way to Pittsburgh, Tony nearly turned round as we went through a very dodgy area and I thought we was going to be mugged as a car stopped in front of us. I was going to say the man at the back (Tony) has the money! Visited Bicycle Heaven, highlight of the trip for Tony. 1000's of vintage and antique bikes. *(Through E-Bay I had had contact several times with Craig).*

We took a bicycle taxi to Gettysburg in time for the 4th July celebrations. *(We met Wiley Drake an evangelical preacher with his own radio and TV show. We didn't like him. I behaved when he, broadcasting live, asked me to say a few words. I just said what we were doing. But at least I could add to my spurious list of achievements that I had appeared on one of those awful religious shows. Only I was excluded from asking for money).*

And then onto Lancaster County (Amish country). If you ever get the chance then go cycling around Amish country, this was so good I don't have the words to describe how fabulous our time spent here was. *(That's a lot of use in a book Anne)* Tony did a fantastic trip tour and we really got to see how Amish people live and work. Very hilly cycling, very hot and sunny but worth every dime. *(No, I didn't charge them).*

Last bit of the trip into Washington D.C.. What a great time we had and a big thank you Tony XXX.

(This was one of my easiest trips and a great time with Anne and Stef, lots of laughs. One downer was that on the return leg I ripped my tendons in my left ankle. The last couple of hundred miles were agony. Resulting in months of operations including having my heel removed and repositioned. But at least it gave me time to plan my next adventure.)

Chapter 19: Death Valley and Mojave Desert

Death Valley was a ride I had always wanted to take, and now, coming up to 72 I was running out of time. I was fascinated by stories of the "Lost 49ers" who during the Gold Rush tried to find a shorter route to the Goldfields of California, but ended up trapped. Although only one man died, they named it "Death Valley" due to the heat, shortage of water and mountainous terrain. Death Valley has the highest temperature ever recorded on the planet at 134F, 56C. It was another thirty years before borax mining commenced at Furnace Creek, and twenty mule teams were needed to haul the white mineral out of the valley. That alone should have alerted me to what I might be up against with respect to going over the mountains surrounding Death Valley. I had already cycled across most of the mountain ranges of the world, so what could there be to fear?

I knew that wild camping was not going to be possible in the National Park, so at least I wouldn't be hauling my camping gear along. Accommodation would be a mix of Casino Hotels and Airbnb.

In 2017 I flew into Las Vegas and the owner of my first Airbnb, Clint, met me at the airport with his truck. It was a room in Clint's and his wife Ann's home just off Blue Diamond Rd, perfect for getting out of Las Vegas and already on the road to Beatty. Needing a couple of extra spares, Clint ran me down to the local bike shop. I began to feel a bit nauseous putting it down to jet lag. Then the pain in my stomach started and I rushed outside to throw up in a drain. Trying to think what I had been eating and another wave of pain came over me. Suddenly something started pushing itself out of me, like a scene from The Alien when a Xenomorph started trying to get out of my groin area, rather than my chest. Abandoning the bike, Clint and the shop owner helped me to a medical centre in the same complex. Checking out my vitals, insurance and credit card were all in order, I was ushered in to see the doctor. After a cursory examination he told me I would need to go straight to hospital and called an ambulance. Being wheeled out of the centre I marvelled at the efficiency of the receptionist who handed me my receipt for $4,600, which included the ambulance, she said, making it sound like a bargain. I was seen straight away at the hospital and diagnosed with a strangulated hernia, or in the USA an incarcerated hernia needing immediate surgery. Talking to the doctor the following day he said the mortality rate is around 20 to 40 percent, and just as well it hadn't occurred while out in the desert.

Clint, a Vietnam veteran and his wife Ann from Vietnam were great and after a short stay in hospital I was discharged to their home. Clint was a freelance film cameraman, and a string of wannabe actors came to the house for him to make a demo film, sent when applying for an audition.

I repacked my bike and shipped it to Portland Oregon, where some family were living. It could remain there ready for my next foray into Death Valley.

A year later I was fit enough to fly out again, and this time I based myself on the outskirts of Las Vegas in an "Airstream" Airbnb caravan and it was close to a Walmart supermarket.

Heading out on Blue Diamond Rd or #160, I didn't get far when I was told I couldn't cycle through the mountain pass because they were blasting, to make the road wider and only vehicles allowed through. Fortunately, there are so many trucks driven in the USA that I managed to find a Chevrolet Truck in the queue that agreed to take me to the other side of the road works. This left me a nice, easy downhill ride into Pahrump and the Saddle West Hotel and Casino. Wandering around the casino, I got talking to Dee, a woman in her late sixties, who said she spent all day, every day, playing one machine. Dee knew she was addicted and spent all her money gambling including putting any winnings back in the machine. She knew what she did was "stupid" it all seemed so sad; she had no family or friends, only ever talking to the casino staff and living in a mobile unit attached to the casino. Anyone playing the "slots" was given food vouchers, otherwise, I think she might have starved. Leaving the next morning and going to the restaurant for breakfast I was amazed to see Dee still sitting at the same machine, having been there all night, now that takes stamina! We had breakfast together, and she wanted to know all about my cycling plans and life, but she was totally reticent about her own life prior to "living" in the casino. I still think about her and hope she is OK.

At this time, there was an election taking place for the Nevada state legislator between Dennis Hof, a brothel owner and a Christian educator. Dennis Hof won with 68% of the votes, even though he had died the previous month. Take from that what you will.

I didn't envisage just how a dead brothel owner would impact on my next overnight accommodation in Crystal, a desert town. Crystal was where Hoff had one of his brothels, totally legal in Nevada. Strangely, prostitution is illegal in Las Vegas while those wanting this kind of service could take one of the mini-buses owned by Hof out to one of his brothels.

I was booked in at "Miss Kathy's Saloon", a five-kilometre detour off the main road into Crystal. At the first junction was a signpost pointing down the street to a brothel. It had been pulled down and smashed to pieces. On to Miss Kathy's Saloon, only to find it closed and deserted. Despite several calls previously to Miss Kathy who had assured me that food and Airbnb accommodation would be available. It was getting late, and being tired, I knew I had no alternative other than staying in this eight-block town. Wandering over to a property that looked inhabited, I ask about Miss Kathy, only to find out she no longer lived there but came and opened up occasionally.

After all, she was nearly eighty. I asked about food and the guy said you might be able to get the chef at the brothel to make you something to eat. First, I needed a place to sleep and went around the back of the saloon where there were several locked rooms. This was to be my first and only breaking and entry escapade. I hadn't realised how good I was at it and soon had the door open without too much damage. Now, time to search for food, reaching Hofs brothel, it was clearly deserted and looked as if it had been ransacked.

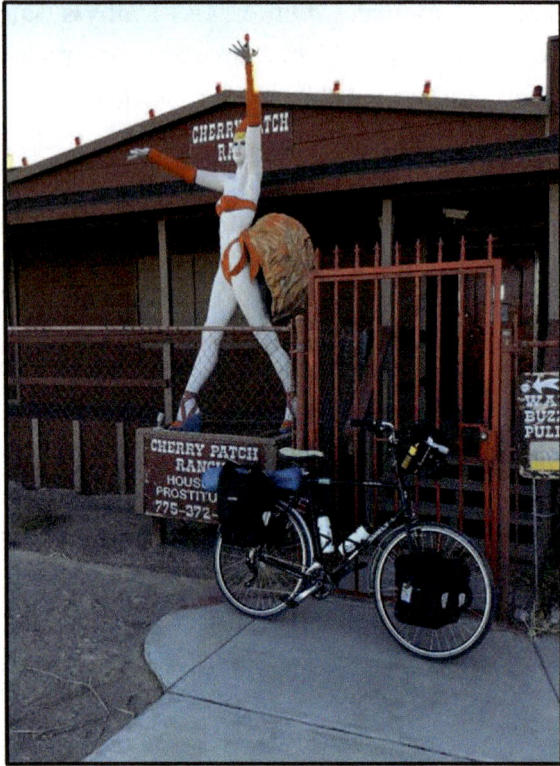

Figure 80 No Chance of A Meal Or Anything Else, Like A Beer.

Fortunately, Miss Kathy had a supply of breakfast oats and syrup, just add boiling water. Four of these meant a full stomach to sleep on and a few more in the morning. I didn't feel I was stealing as I had paid for my stay with Miss Kathy through Airbnb.

Long, straight, smooth roads through the Mojave Desert with little foliage. There were substantial hills set away from the road and occasionally you would see a hole with spoil out front where a prospector had hoped to hit a lode. I was heading for Area 5, the supposed centre for Aliens. What would be their reason for making Area 5 their preferred landing point? All that was there was a rest area, restaurant and a brothel. Oh and of course the USA's nuclear

172

weapons testing site. Was that it? Or the brothel? Had I cracked the mystery? I stopped for a meal with a window seat overlooking the entrance to the brothel. There were some odd-looking men visiting but none that looked like a space alien.

Next stop, Longstreet Casino on the Nevada/Californian border. From the Casino I could see some narrow tracks heading away at 45 degrees, this would save me quite some distance. The only problem when trying to find out about them was that no-one could understand where I wanted to go. They had never heard of Beatty. Turns out the TT is pronounced as DD. It reminded me that some years previously, my wife, Pauline, entered a shop in New Hampshire and asked for a bottle of water. No one serving could comprehend what she was saying, culminating in Pauline being asked, "Ma'am is English your first language?" Already frustrated and in her best haughty voice replied "I am English!"

I planned to stay in Beatty for a couple of days, visiting Rhyolite, a mining ghost town up in the Bullfrog Hills. I remember there was a house built from discarded beer bottles which I had visited several years previously. It is still standing while many of the more traditionally built properties are falling apart.

Time to head into Death Valley, reaching Daylight Pass at 4,317ft above sea level, it's a thrilling 27-mile downhill ride to Furnace Creek and Death Valley at 282 feet below sea level. I enjoyed the free-wheel ride with no thoughts about having to climb back out at some point!

Basing myself at Furnace Creek, I took several trips out to the various points of interest in the valley and back to the swimming pool in the afternoon, heaven. Unusually for me, I hadn't done any research into any of the rides, because…OK, it's time to come clean, on the day I reached Furnace Creek, I took the opportunity to use the washing machine, dumping all my clothes out of my pannier straight in. The moment I set the machine going and heard clunk clunk clunk I remembered I had put my tablet in with my clothes to keep it safe in case of a fall. Impossible to open the lid, I had to wait until the end of the cycle, and sure enough, my tablet was terminal. This was my only means of checking out the roads using Google Maps, and I nearly paid the penalty for not being aware of the

174

terrain. Artist Pallet, I wouldn't have attempted it if I had known how brutal the hills were, and with the heat, I struggled to make it out, pushing uphill and feeling ill in the heat. If I had only done the ride in reverse, Daylight Pass is close to 3000 ft lower.

A bit sad to leave this wonderfully desolate area, but I needed to move on. I left early the next day, knowing what steep climbs lay ahead. I was heading for the Death Valley Junction and the Amargosa Opera House. The 190 goes past Zabriskie Point, where a short hike takes you up to views over The Devils Playground. The ride up to the summit at just under 7,000 feet was a struggle, and the heat was starting to get to me. Even on the descents, I was finding it hard. It was with great relief that I reached the junction with the Amargosa Valley.

Figure 81 Amargosa Hotel

I stayed longer than planned at the Amargosa Opera House. What an amazing place in the middle of the desert to have an opera house and the history to go with it. Built in the 1920s, the Opera House is still used for performing arts. Amargosa was the trailhead where borax was dragged up from the valley bottom to be loaded onto trains. I now understand why they needed twenty mules for each load after today's ride.

I planned to go to Tecopa, where they were holding a mini–Burning Man Music festival, and then follow the Old Spanish Trail back to Las Vegas.

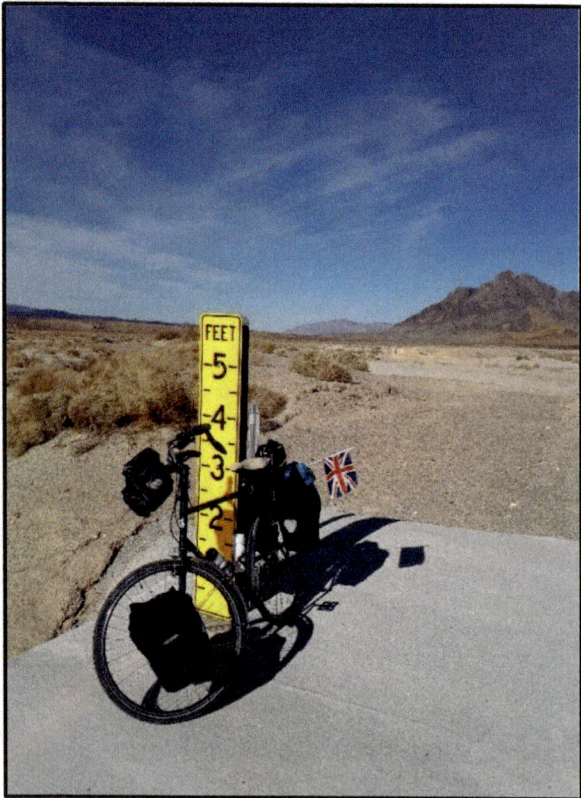

Figure 82 I Guess It Does Rain Sometimes

At Tecopa I had lined up an Airbnb caravan right in the centre of the festival, which was ok as, although the music went on all night, after ten the town ordinance forbids loud music and everyone continued dancing through the night wearing headphones. I thought before heading along the Old Spanish Highway I'd ride a couple of miles just to see why everyone was telling me it was only passable in a four-wheel drive truck. After an hour, I knew why, the surface had deep cracks that your wheels keep getting stuck in. I decided this was not going to work, and so the following day back tracked to Amargosa Opera House and Longstreet Casino all feeling like old friends now. It was a fairly easy ride back to Pahrump and the Saddle West Casino, where sure enough my friend Dee was still sitting at the same machine.

The final day still meant I had to hitch a lift past where they were blasting out the new road, but I was pleased to reach my Airstream Airbnb.

With two bags full of serviceable clothes, I didn't want to take them home. The Airbnb owner, Bill, told me there was a donation point in Walmart's car park for homeless people. Walking around the massive car park and unable to find where to leave the clothes I asked a guy if he knew where the homeless clothes drop off was. He replied, "Sorry, no, I don't, but here's five dollars if it will help." Later, taking a long, hard look at myself in a mirror, I saw this 72-year-old haggard-looking old man, with a long straggly beard and greying long hair bleached in the sun and a deep sun tan to go with it. To add to the vision, my tatterdemalion, shorts and tee shirt were both bleached.

On the flight home I thought about my trip and realised I had found it much harder than any of my previous rides, and that I was struggling with the heat for the first time. I already had difficulties getting up off the ground, hence I decided not to camp and had carried a lightweight folding chair for any rest breaks off the bike. I sadly knew then that this would be the last long haul bicycle trek I would do.

Writing this at seventy-eight and looking back at the Death Valley ride, it was probably not the most sensible trip to have done at my age. My bike is still in the box I used on the flight home and is never likely to be unpacked.

THE END

Printed in Dunstable, United Kingdom